GOVERNMENT PROCEDURES AND OPERATIONS

IRS EXAMINATION OF TAX-EXEMPT ORGANIZATIONS

ANALYSIS AND PERSPECTIVE

GOVERNMENT PROCEDURES AND OPERATIONS

Additional books in this series can be found on Nova's website under the Series tab.

Additional e-books in this series can be found on Nova's website under the e-book tab.

GOVERNMENT PROCEDURES AND OPERATIONS

IRS EXAMINATION OF TAX-EXEMPT ORGANIZATIONS

ANALYSIS AND PERSPECTIVE

AUSTIN H. WHITE
EDITOR

nova publishers
New York

Library of Congress Cataloging-in-Publication Data

ISBN: 978-1-63484-471-0

Published by Nova Science Publishers, Inc. † New York

CONTENTS

PREFACE

The Exempt Organizations (EO) unit within the Tax Exempt and Government Entities (TE/GE) division at the Internal Revenue Service (IRS) reviews organizations' applications for tax-exempt status to determine whether to grant status and oversees existing exempt organizations' compliance with the tax code. To identify exempt organizations for possible examination, EO uses a variety of information sources: for example, EO receives referrals of exempt organization noncompliance from third parties, such as the public, and other parts of IRS. This book describes these processes and assesses the adequacy of examination selection controls.

In: IRS Examination …
Editor: Austin H. White

ISBN: 978-1-63484-471-0

Chapter 1

IRS Examination Selection: Internal Controls for Exempt Organization Selection Should Be Strengthened*

United States Government Accountability Office

Why GAO Did This Study

IRS examines tax-exempt organizations to enforce their compliance with the tax code. Examinations can result in assessment of taxes or revocation of tax-exempt status, among other things.

GAO was asked to review IRS's criteria and processes for selecting exempt organizations for examination. This report (1) describes these processes and (2) assesses the adequacy of examination selection controls.

GAO reviewed IRS criteria, processes, and controls for selecting organizations for examination and spoke with IRS officials; assessed whether IRS controls followed *Standards for Internal Control in the Federal Government*; reviewed random probability samples from two populations of examination files; and conducted tests on populations and random probability samples from three databases used in EO examination selection to determine the adequacy of EO's control implementation (for files closed in fiscal year

---

* This is an edited, reformatted and augmented version of a United States Government Accountability Office publication, No. GAO-15-514, dated July 2015.

2014). GAO also conducted eight focus groups on internal controls topics with EO staff who conduct research or make examination selection decisions.

WHAT GAO RECOMMENDS

GAO is recommending that IRS take 10 actions to improve selection control design and implementation, such as ensuring that all selection procedures are included in the IRM and thus subject to executive management approval, and developing additional examination selection monitoring procedures. IRS generally agreed with the recommendations.

WHAT GAO FOUND

The Exempt Organizations (EO) unit within the Tax Exempt and Government Entities (TE/GE) division at the Internal Revenue Service (IRS) reviews organizations' applications for tax-exempt status to determine whether to grant status and oversees existing exempt organizations' compliance with the tax code. To identify exempt organizations for possible examination, EO uses a variety of information sources: for example, EO receives referrals of exempt organization noncompliance from third parties, such as the public, and other parts of IRS.

EO uses various controls intended to help it select exempt organizations for examination, in an effort to adhere to TE/GE's mission of "applying the tax law with integrity and fairness to all." For example, EO maintains well-documented procedures for several examination selection processes in the Internal Revenue Manual (IRM), IRS's primary, official source of instructions to staff; staff can deviate from procedures that are included in the IRM only with executive management approval. In focus groups, EO staff generally told GAO that these procedures were valuable tools to help them administer the tax law.

However, there are several areas where EO's controls were not well designed or implemented. The control deficiencies GAO found increase the risk that EO could select organizations for examination in an unfair manner—for example, based on an organization's religious, educational, political, or other views. Examples of internal control deficiencies GAO found include the following:

- **Staff could deviate from procedures for some selection processes without executive management approval.** GAO found that procedures for some processes—such as applying selection criteria to organizations under consideration for review— are not included in the IRM, as required by IRS policy. As a result, staff are not required to obtain executive management approval to deviate from these procedures. This increases the risk of unfair selection of organizations' returns for examination.
- **EO management does not consistently monitor selection decisions.** GAO found that IRS does not consistently monitor examinations and database files to ensure that selection decisions are documented and approved, to help ensure fairness. GAO's review of examination files found that approval of some selection decisions was not documented, as required by EO procedures. For example, GAO's analysis of a sample of files suggests that an estimated 12 to 34 percent of cases where staff initially selected an organization for examination, but ultimately decided not to perform the examination, were missing the indication of management approval of the final decision, as required in the IRM. Continuous monitoring is an element of internal control; EO management has not been conducting sufficient monitoring to ensure that required approvals were taking place.

ABBREVIATIONS

EO	Exempt Organizations
EOCA	Exempt Organizations Compliance Area
IRC	Internal Revenue Code
IRM	Internal Revenue Manual
IRS	Internal Revenue Service
RCCMS	Reporting Compliance Case Management System
RICS	Returns Inventory and Classification System
TE/GE	Tax Exempt and Government Entities

* * *

July 13, 2015
The Honorable Charles E. Grassley
Chairman

Committee on Judiciary
United States Senate

The Honorable Peter Roskam
Chairman
Subcommittee on Oversight
Committee on Ways and Means
United States
House of Representatives

The Honorable Charles W. Boustany
House of Representatives

There are 1.6 million tax-exempt organizations in the United States. These organizations have varied purposes and missions, ranging from small social services groups to large nonprofit health systems. Taken as a whole, exempt organizations represent at least 5 percent of gross domestic product.[1]

An exempt organization must be organized for one of the exempt purposes in the Internal Revenue Code (IRC)—such as providing charity, social welfare, programs for veterans, or furthering the interests of the organization's membership—and must operate in accordance with that purpose. Under the IRC, exempt organizations generally are not subject to federal income taxes. For example, contributions received from sources such as individual donations or grants are not taxable. However, exempt organizations are required to pay employment taxes. In addition, they may be required to pay taxes on unrelated business income, such as from personal property rentals or web site advertising, and most domestic private foundations must pay excise taxes on net investment income.[2]

The Exempt Organizations (EO) unit within the Tax Exempt and Government Entities (TE/GE) division at the Internal Revenue Service (IRS) oversees exempt organizations' compliance with the tax code. EO reviews organizations' applications for exempt status and determines whether to grant it. Additionally, EO conducts examinations, which are reviews of the activities and finances of exempt organizations to determine whether they are operating in accordance with their exempt purposes, and have paid taxes they owe.[3] If IRS finds noncompliance, it may impose excise taxes for certain types of violations, or—if the violations are serious enough—it may revoke an organization's exempt status. In addition, IRS can assess taxes if an organization has not fully paid employment taxes or taxes on unrelated business income, as well as advise organizations on future tax compliance. In fiscal year 2014, IRS closed 8,084 examinations of exempt organizations.

You asked us to review IRS's criteria and processes for selecting exempt organizations for examination. This report (1) describes the processes for selecting exempt organizations for examination, and (2) assesses the adequacy of the controls (including procedures) for selecting examination cases that EO uses to achieve TE/GE's stated mission of "applying the tax law with integrity and fairness to all."[4]

For the first objective, we reviewed IRS documents that describe the criteria, processes, and controls for selecting exempt organization returns for examination. These documents included relevant sections of the IRC, regulations, the Internal Revenue Manual (IRM), EO procedures and training documents, worksheets to guide examinations and reviews, and summaries of processes prepared by EO officials. We also interviewed IRS officials responsible for overseeing each process. In addition, we obtained data from the following IRS databases: Return Inventory Classification System (RICS), Referrals database, Exempt Organizations Compliance Area (EOCA) database, and EOCA Classification database. The databases contain information on initiated and closed examinations, classification of referrals, and other reviews that can lead to an exempt organization's return(s) being selected for examination.[5] Based on our testing of the data and review of documentation and interviews, we determined that these data were reliable for the purposes of this report.

For the second objective, we reviewed EO's examination selection procedures and the related internal controls EO uses to help TE/GE achieve its stated mission of "enforcing the tax law with integrity and fairness to all." [6] We then assessed whether these procedures adhered to *Standards for Internal Control in the Federal Government.*[7] We also conducted six focus groups with selected EO staff who are responsible for selecting, or doing research to help select, exempt organization returns for examination, and two focus groups of selected EO staff who conduct examinations. We asked questions on internal control related topics, such as the clarity of EO procedures and the adequacy of training to apply these procedures. We used NVivo qualitative data analysis software to conduct a content analysis of themes from the focus groups.

To assess how well EO implemented its procedures and controls and applied examination selection criteria, we used IRM sections, EO procedures documents, and other documents as criteria. We reviewed databases used to document examination selection decisions and random probability samples of database files and examination files. We used the results of those reviews to determine whether selected controls were implemented effectively. We also reviewed a non-generalizable sample of 11 projects that were active during fiscal year 2014.[8] We selected those projects to include projects of various sizes (based on numbers of returns examined) and time frames, and we included politically sensitive projects and some projects that relied on data queries of Form 990, *Return of Organization Exempt From Income Tax*. We reviewed the project files for each project to test whether the documentation—such as development and approval of examination selection criteria—followed project development procedures. Finally, we interviewed EO officials about the processes and controls, and to discuss any potential deficiencies we identified.

We designed uniform data collection instruments for our file and database reviews to consistently capture information on the completeness of required documentation and approvals related to case selection. IRS verified the criteria we used in our instruments. To ensure accuracy, two analysts reviewed each file or database entry we assessed, and reconciled any differences in responses. We then analyzed the results of these data collection efforts to identify main themes and develop summary findings.

We conducted this performance audit from May 2014 to July 2015 in accordance with generally accepted government auditing standards. Those standards require that we plan and perform the audit to obtain sufficient, appropriate evidence to provide a reasonable basis for our findings and conclusions based on our audit objectives. We believe that the evidence obtained provides a reasonable basis for our findings and conclusions based on our audit objectives. More detailed information on our scope and methodology appears in appendix I.

BACKGROUND

The tax code provides for 35 different categories of exempt organizations, each covering one or more types of permissible activities. The majority of these organizations are covered by section 501 of the IRC. Section 501 includes private foundations and public charities, as well as other organizations, such as social welfare organizations, business leagues, and veterans' organizations.[9] However, other types of entities are also wholly or partially tax exempt, such as farmers' cooperatives and political organizations,[10] as are education-oriented programs such as educational savings accounts and tuition programs.[11]

Most organizations seeking exemption must submit an application to IRS. 12 If the information in the application meets the requirements for tax exempt status, IRS will issue a determination letter approving tax exempt status. Tax exempt organizations are generally not required to file an income tax return. Instead, if an organization normally has $50,000 or more in gross receipts, and meets other requirements, it must annually file one of three versions of the Form 990 information return, which require information on employees, revenue and income, assets and liabilities, program activities, and compensation.[13] Most organizations that fall below the gross receipt threshold of $50,000 and need not file a Form 990 information return are required instead to file an electronic postcard, Form 990-N, which asks for names and contacts associated with the organization, and confirmation of the organization's annual gross receipts.

During examinations, EO reviews a specific return—such as a Form 990 or employment tax return—as well as the organization's activities. There can be open examinations on one organization spanning several years, or related returns for a single tax period for that same organization. Some examinations are a result of compliance projects that IRS initiates to identify areas of noncompliance or address known areas of noncompliance. For example, a project on gaming in charity fundraising activities, an activity often conducted by veterans organizations, led to a relatively high examination rate—compared with other rates by tax-exempt status—for those organizations in fiscal year 2014. Table 1 shows the examination rate by organization exempt status for fiscal year 2014.

Table 1. Examination Coverage Rate by Type of Tax-exempt Status, Fiscal Year 2014

Type of tax-exempt status	Examination coverage rate
Charitable organizations, 501(c)(3)	0.66
Public charities	0.68
Private foundations	0.52
Social welfare organization, 501(c)(4)	0.71
Business league/trade association, 501(c)(6)	0.41
Fraternal societies, 501(c)(8) and 501(c)(10)	0.71
Social clubs, 501(c)(7)	1.64
Labor organization, 501(c)(5), agricultural/ horticulture organization	0.34
Veterans organizations, 501(c)(19)	2.49

Table 1. (Continued)

Type of tax-exempt status	Examination coverage rate
Political organizations, 527	0.06
Other 501(c) organizations	1.08
Other (related individual and for-profit entities)	—[a]
Overall	**0.73**

Source: IRS Return Inventory Classification System data, end of fiscal year 2014, and TE/GE Research.

Notes: IRS defines the examination coverage rate as the number of examinations closed in the fiscal year for the population (type of organization status), expressed as a percentage of the corresponding number of returns filed in the previous calendar year.

[a]This examination coverage rate is not included because it is not calculated using a population of exempt organizations in the denominator.

EO Process for Selecting Exempt Organizations for Examination

EO's process for selecting returns for examination is complex and includes multiple steps (see figure 1). Referrals, which are complaints against exempt organizations submitted to EO, involve additional steps; they are excluded from figure 1 and discussed later in this report.

EO uses a variety of sources to identify exempt organizations for possible examination, and conducts review steps that filter out some organizations. Through ongoing programs, time-limited projects, and data queries, EO identifies organizations with characteristics that may pose high noncompliance risks. Referrals point EO toward particular organizations that may be noncompliant. In addition, EO reviews organizations' claims for tax refunds and examines those that are questionable; EO selects examination cases for training examiners; and some cases are selected based on programs run by other parts of IRS that relate to exempt organizations. EO also identifies some organizations for examination in the course of conducting other examinations. For a breakdown of closed examinations by source during fiscal year 2014, see table 2. Primary examination sources are listed in the rows, and examinations that are initiated based on other examinations are reflected in the third and fourth columns.

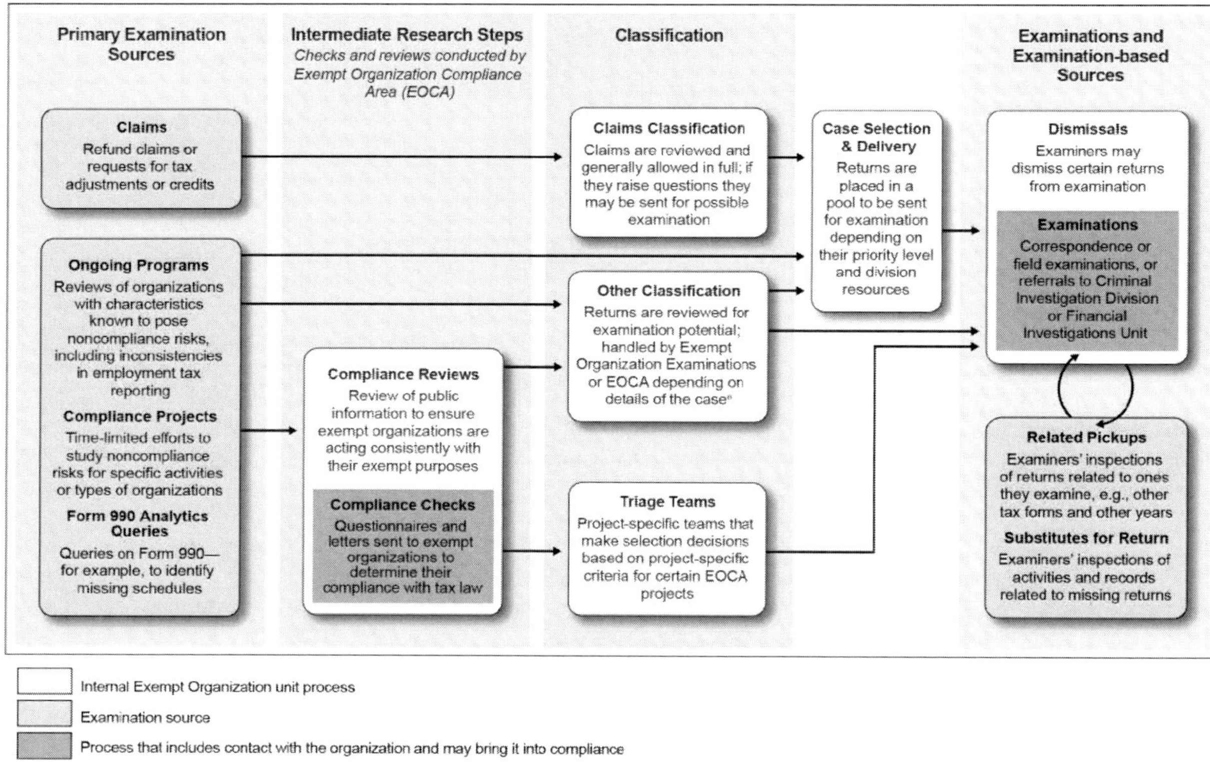

Source: GAO analysis of IRS guidance. | GAO-15-514.

Notes: Some additional paths are possible but not common. For example, some compliance review cases are sent straight to case selection and delivery without being sent first for classification or to triage teams. Also, compliance check cases can be sent for compliance reviews, and vice versa.

Selection based on referrals, training, and work for other IRS divisions is not illustrated here.

[a]Cases that had compliance checks are classified by EOCA. Cases that had compliance reviews are classified by Exempt Organization Examinations. If a case classified by EOCA meets certain criteria, it may be forwarded to Exempt Organization Examinations classification. Cases that had neither compliance reviews nor compliance checks may be classified by either group, depending on the details of the case. The two groups have different criteria and procedures. Cases classified by EOCA as having examination potential are generally sent for correspondence examinations conducted by EOCA. Cases classified by Exempt Organization Examinations as having examination potential are sent to Case Selection and Delivery and are generally conducted as field examinations.

Figure 1. Exempt Organization Examination Selection (Excluding Referrals).

Table 2. Closed Exempt Organization Examinations by Source, Fiscal Year 2014

Primary Source	Primary examinations	Related pickups	Substitutes for return	Totals
Ongoing programs	1,742	233	307	2,282
Form 990 analytics queries	1,233	254	250	1,737
Referrals	993	279	358	1,630
Compliance projects	724	198	256	1,178
Work for other IRS divisions	238	415	10	663
Claimsa	480	15	5	500
Training	39	20	35	94
Total	5,449	1,414	1,221	8,084

Source: GAO analysis of IRS data from the Return Inventory Classification System, the end of fiscal year 2014. | GAO-15-514

Note:

[a]Most claims are allowable and are processed and issued in full. Claims that raise questions may result in an examination.

EO Identifies Groups of Organizations with Characteristics That Pose Noncompliance Risks

Ongoing programs.[14] Every year, EO identifies organizations with characteristics that are known to pose a risk of noncompliance. For example, through a document matching program, EO matches wages reported on Form W-2, *Wage and Tax Statement*, to those reported on exempt organizations' employment tax returns; organizations with mismatches have an increased probability of noncompliance.[15] Additionally, ongoing programs are used in EO's oversight role. For example, EO performs annual reviews of a random sample of organizations that recently received favorable determination letters to check if the organizations are current with their filing requirements and are operating in accordance with their tax exempt purposes.

Compliance projects are time-limited efforts to study noncompliance risks. Through compliance projects, EO identifies specific areas of potential noncompliance (such as fundraising) or specific types of organizations (such as community foundations), selects and reviews a subset of relevant organizations, and addresses any noncompliance it finds. Compliance projects identify organizations for review using data queries, random samples, and/or nonprobability samples. A committee of TE/GE officials, including EO managers and analysts, has historically been tasked with developing new compliance projects and obtaining approval from EO executives.

Primary Examination Sources

Ongoing Programs
Reviews of organizations with characteristics known to pose noncompliance risks, including inconsistencies in employment tax reporting

Compliance Projects
Time-limited efforts to study noncompliance risks for specific activities or types of organizations

Form 990 Analytics Queries
Queries based on the various versions of Form 990

Source: GAO analysis of IRS guidance. | GAO-15-514

Projects that identify areas of significant noncompliance—based on the nature of the issues involved and the number of examinations that result in tax assessments or organization status changes—become part of EO's ongoing programs. However, in the past few years, EO has decreased its focus on compliance projects and developed a new focus on Form 990 analytics queries (see below).

Form 990 analytics queries identify organizations for review with data queries on Form 990, *Return of Organization Exempt from Income Tax*. For example, some queries check for missing Form 990 schedules that should be filed, based on boxes checked on Form 990 or Form 990 responses above certain dollar thresholds. To assure alignment with IRS objectives, EO is in the process of aligning Form 990 analytics queries with five focus areas that correspond to agency-wide IRS objectives.[16] EO initiated the Form 990 analytics strategy in 2010, and developed and began testing about 150 data queries by 2012. Of the original 150 Form 990 analytics queries, EO had completed testing for 11 and was in the process of testing 20 others, as of April 2015. Successful queries are run on an ongoing basis. As with compliance projects, queries that identify areas of significant noncompliance—based on the nature of the issues involved and the number of examinations that result in tax assessments or organization status changes—become part of EO's ongoing programs.

Referrals Identify Particular Organizations that May Be Noncompliant

Referrals are complaints of exempt organization noncompliance made by third parties, including the public and other parts of EO and IRS. (Although referrals can be made from sources within EO, 90 percent of referrals are from sources external to EO.) Referrals will be discussed in greater detail later in this report.

Some Examinations Are Conducted for Other IRS Divisions, and Some Are Used for Training

Examinations Conducted in Conjunction with Other IRS Divisions

EO conducts some examinations as part of programs managed by other divisions of IRS. For example, EO conducts some examinations for the Global High Wealth program, managed by IRS's Large Business and International Division, which monitors high wealth individuals and the networks of enterprises and entities they control. Additionally, EO conducts some examinations of exempt organizations for the National Research Program, an IRS-wide effort to develop and monitor measures of taxpayer compliance run by IRS's Office of Research, Analysis, and Statistics. IRS initiated a National Research Program study on employment tax noncompliance in 2010, focusing on Form 941, *Employer's Quarterly Federal Tax Return*, for tax years 2008, 2009, and 2010.

Training examinations, used for training examiners, are identified through database queries selecting for lower-grade cases with compliance issues, and cases with particular topics relevant to training.

Most Claims Are Allowed in Full, but Some Lead to Examinations

Claims are exempt organizations' requests for tax refunds, adjustments of tax paid, or credits not previously reported or allowed. For example, recognition of tax-exempt status occurs after an organization was formed, effective to the formation date. As a result, an organization can file a claim for refund of income taxes paid for the period for which its exempt status is recognized. Most claims are allowed in full, but claims that raise questions may be considered for examination.

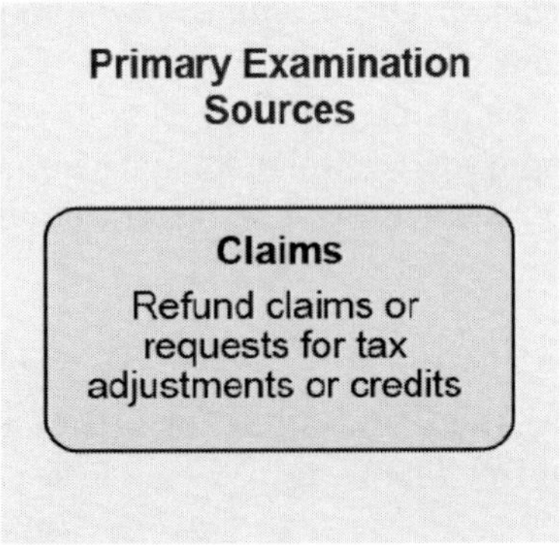

Source: GAO analysis of IRS guidance. | GAO-15-514

EO Identifies Some Organizations to Examine Based on Other Examinations

In the course of examining an exempt organization's tax return, EO examiners may become aware of other tax returns that are at risk for noncompliance and should be examined. EO has two sets of procedures in place for opening examinations on those returns when this occurs.

Related pickups. Examiners may expand the examination of a return to include the organization's tax returns for prior or subsequent years. They may also expand the examination to include different forms filed by the organization—for example, by expanding the examination of a Form 990 to include Form 941, *Employer's Quarterly Federal Tax Return*.

Examination staff must obtain manager approval for these examinations.

Substitutes for return. When beginning an examination of a particular tax return, EO examiners check whether the organization is current in its filing requirements for all its returns. If EO examiners find that a return is missing, and are unable to secure the return through contact with the organization, they may prepare a blank, "dummy" return called a substitute for return (necessary because IRS tracks its examinations based on returns). The organization's related activities, records, and/or documents may then be examined.

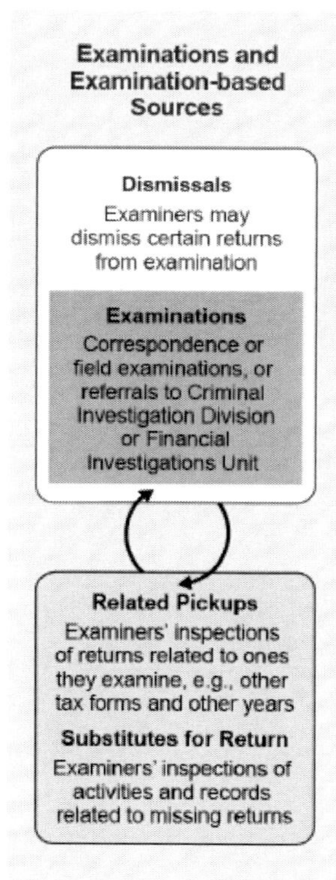

Source: GAO analysis of IRS guidance. | GAO-15-514

EO Conducts Research on Some Organizations as Part of the Selection Process

For some cases, EO's Exempt Organizations Compliance Area (EOCA) may conduct a compliance check or compliance review, processes that can serve as intermediate research steps (see table 3). Some organizations are filtered out through these steps, some are brought into compliance and do not require further work, and some are sent for classification (see below). Other cases are not sent for intermediate research and are sent directly for classification, or directly to Case Selection and Delivery, which manages the pool of returns that may be sent for examination.

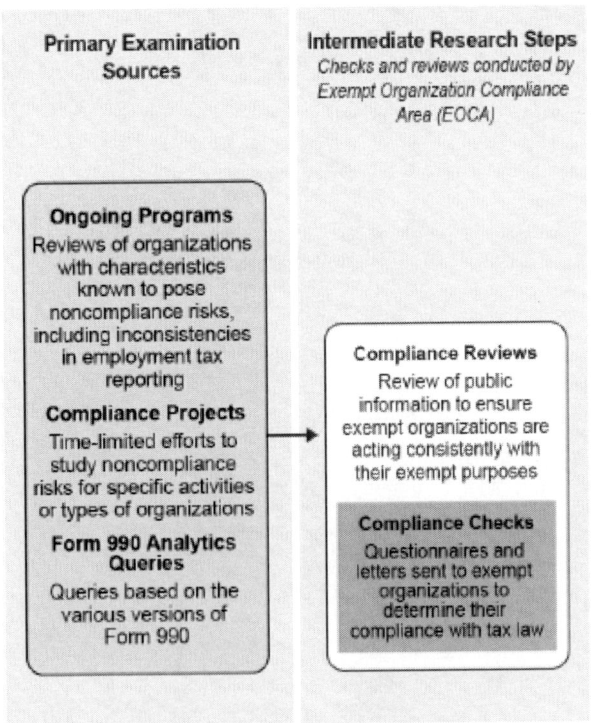

Source: GAO analysis of IRS guidance. | GAO-15-514

Table 3. Compliance Checks and Compliance Reviews Closed in Fiscal Year 2014

	Cases closed	Delinquent returns secured	Organizations referred for examination	Examinations closed based on this type of case[a]
Compliance checks	3,237	913	102	1,254
Compliance reviews[b]	2,005	N/A	152	241
Total Cases	**5,242**	**913**	**254**	**1,495**

Source: GAO and IRS analyses of IRS data. | GAO-15-514

Notes:

[a]An organization referred for examination based on a single compliance check or compliance review may be subject to examinations on multiple tax returns. Examinations counted in the final column are based on the types of cases listed, but do not necessarily result from the specific cases counted in the other columns, because compliance checks and compliance reviews closed in a particular fiscal year can result in examinations that close in future fiscal years.

[b]Excludes mandatory reviews conducted in accordance with Section 9007(c) of the Patient Protection and Affordable Care Act. EOCA conducts mandatory reviews of hospitals that wish to retain or obtain tax exempt status under requirements imposed by the Patient Protection and Affordable Care Act. Pub. L. No. 111-148, § 9007, 124 Stat. 119 (2010), § 9007(a). Section 9007(a) imposed new requirements that a hospital organization must meet to qualify for tax exemption in tax years beginning after March 23, 2010. 26 U.S.C. § 501(r). The Secretary of the Treasury or the Secretary's delegate must review the community benefit activities of each hospital organization to which this section applies, at least once every 3 years. Pub. L. 111-148, 124 Stat. 857, § 9007(c). These mandatory reviews are outside the scope of this report. EOCA conducts these reviews as compliance reviews.

Compliance checks involve contact with an exempt organization through a letter or questionnaire. For example, in fiscal year 2014, EOCA sent compliance check letters to organizations that did not file a required Form 990, and to organizations that reported certain types of income on their Form 990 but did not file related required forms. These contacts are a form of education for an organization and can result in the organization coming into compliance with requirements—for example, by filing a required return. Compliance checks may also be used to determine whether an organization is adhering to record-keeping requirements, and they are used for document matching cases.

With some compliance checks, the contact is sufficient to bring an organization into compliance, or to determine that it was already in compliance. Other cases may be sent to EOCA's classification group or a triage team (see below), which determines which cases meet criteria for examination.

Compliance reviews do not involve contacting the reviewed organization. EOCA conducts research using IRS data, external databases, and publicly available information, including information on the Internet.[17] Items reviewed may include tax returns, applications for exemption, and websites. For example, compliance reviews are used for the program mentioned above that reviews organizations that were recently granted exempt status, to determine whether they are now operating in accordance with their exempt purposes.[18]

EO May Use Claims Classifiers, Other Classifiers, and Triage Teams to Determine Which Returns Have Examination Potential

Some cases identified through a compliance project may be sent straight to Case Selection and Delivery, the pool of returns that may be sent for possible examination (see below). For other cases, an intermediate research step may or may not be conducted (see above), and the next step is classification, a review of the examination potential of a return.

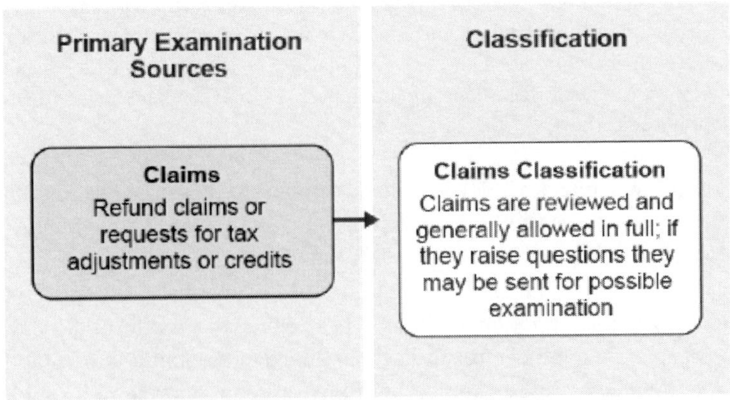

Source: GAO analysis of IRS guidance. | GAO-15-514

Claims Classification. Classifiers apply their experience and technical expertise to determine whether a claim is allowable by reviewing taxpayer documentation. With management approval, claims classifiers recommend processing refunds, credits, or adjustments for claims which are clearly allowable, as most claims are. Claims that raise questions are sent for possible examination.

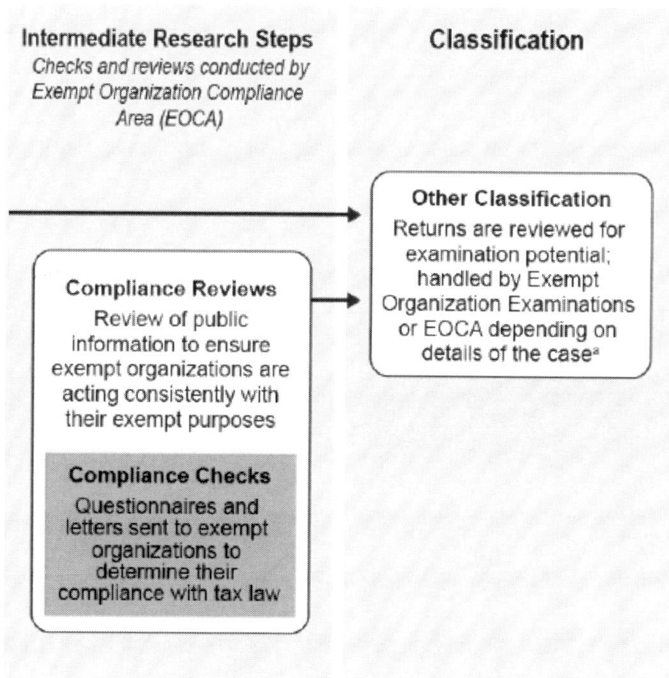

Source: GAO analysis of IRS guidance. | GAO-15-514

Other Classification. Classification of most non-claims cases is done by experienced examiners who conduct further research on an organization. They decide which returns to filter out and which to send forward for possible examination, based on their professional judgment of the likelihood of noncompliance and the significance of the identified issues. Returns are classified by one of two groups, EOCA classification and Exempt Organizations Examinations classification, depending on how the case originated and the details of the case. The two groups use different criteria and procedures, but have similar functions and results; classification by either group may result in a correspondence examination, a field examination, or accepting a return as filed and filtering it out from further review.[19]

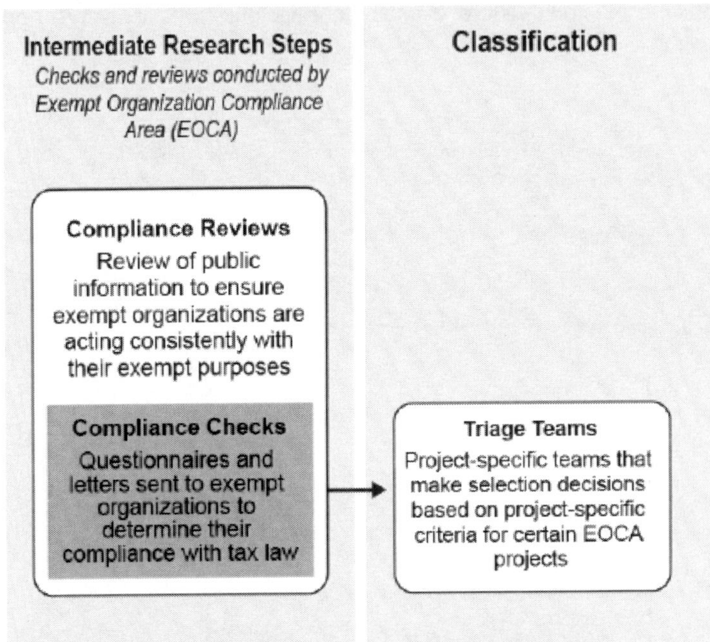

Source: GAO analysis of IRS guidance. | GAO-15-514

Triage Teams. For some EOCA compliance projects, examination selection decisions are made using project-specific criteria applied by project-specific teams, called triage teams, instead of through the usual classification groups. For example, compliance projects that use questionnaires may have triage teams compare questionnaire responses with Form 990 data to select organizations for examination. Triage teams look at the compliance check or compliance review results and apply the project-specific criteria to determine which returns to filter out, and which to send forward for possible examination.

Returns Selected for Potential Examination May or May not Be Sent to Examiners, Depending on Resources

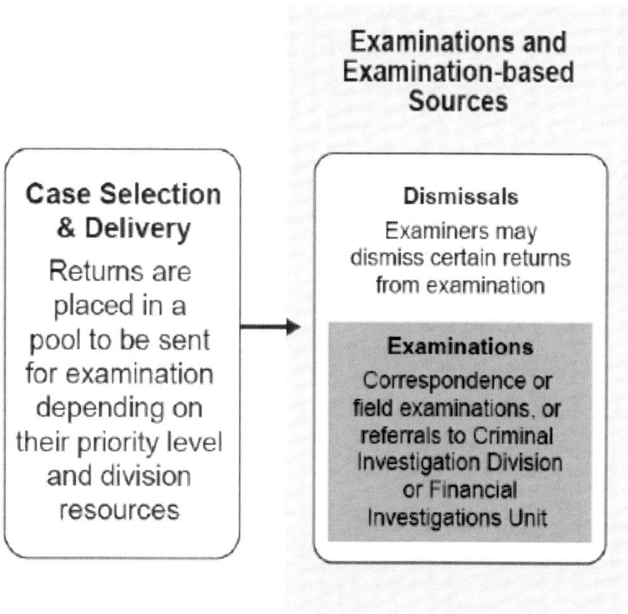

Source: GAO analysis of IRS guidance. | GAO-15-514

Case Selection and Delivery. After identification of organizations for possible examination, and after any intermediate research steps and classification, most returns that are selected for possible examination are sent to EO's Case Selection and Delivery unit. (Returns that were classified by EOCA generally skip this step and may be sent straight to examination by EOCA examiners.) At Case Selection and Delivery, the returns become part of a pool of returns that may be sent for examination. Claims that raise questions (see above) are sent for examination. High-priority and certain other referrals (discussed below) are also sent for examination, according to EO officials. Aside from these referrals and claims, decisions are made based on available resources.[20] Different examinations must be conducted by different grades of examination staff, depending on the nature of the issues involved and the level of income on the return; large and complex organizations are examined through EO's Team Examination Program.[21] Additionally, field examinations generally involve in-person contact and so must be conducted in the geographic area of the exempt organization. Examination offices tell the Case Selection and Delivery unit the grades of examiners available. The unit then sends returns to the offices based on those grades and, in the case of field exams, on the locations of the offices. In fiscal year 2014, 93 percent of returns sent to the Case Selection and Delivery Unit were ultimately sent to examination offices.

Examiners and Managers Make the Final Decision on Whether to Conduct an Examination

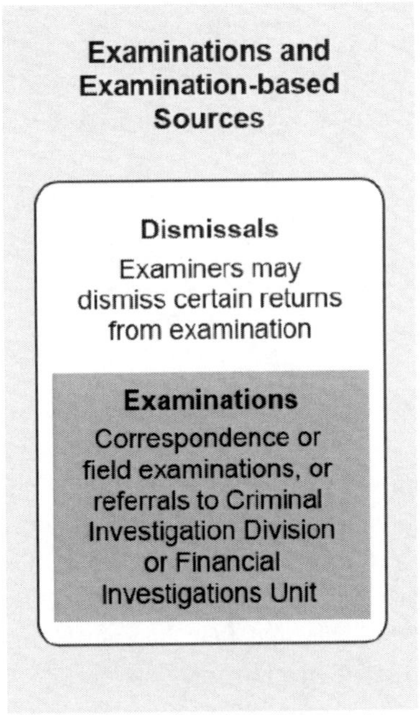

Source: GAO analysis of IRS guidance. | GAO-15-514

Dismissals. After selected returns arrive at examination offices, managers and examiners conduct risk assessments on the returns. They may choose not to conduct the examinations, if returns seem to pose limited noncompliance risk or for other reasons. In this report we use the term "dismissed" to refer to such returns.[22] There were 1,858 returns dismissed in fiscal year 2014, for reasons summarized in table 4. The most frequent reason for dismissing a return was that the return was approaching its statute of limitations; IRS must ensure there is adequate time to complete the examination.[23] Other reasons for dismissal included lack of examination potential, and finding no concerns with a claim for a tax refund. A manager may make the decision to dismiss a return if it has not yet been assigned to an examiner. Examiners who identify returns that they believe should be dismissed are required to fill out a form stating the reason and have that form signed by their manager.

Table 4. Reasons for Dismissed Examinations, Fiscal Year 2014

Reason	Percentage of examinations dismissed
Expiring statute of limitations	37
Returns with no examination potential for other reasons[a]	32
Claims allowed in full	23
No large, unusual, or questionable items	5
Lack of resources	3

Source: RICS data. | GAO-15-514

NOTES:

[a]Examples of other reasons are the examination being unlikely to result in a material change, the examination of a prior year return resulting in no change, and the organization having already taken steps to correct a reported issue.

EO Processes Thousands of Referrals on Potential Noncompliance Each Year

EO has special procedures for processing referrals—complaints of potential noncompliance of exempt organizations—and selecting organizations for possible examination based on referrals. Referrals are the third largest source of EO examinations. EO receives referrals from many sources. They may originate externally—most commonly from the general public—or from other IRS divisions that identify potential noncompliance. Figure 2 summarizes the sources of referrals received in fiscal year 2014; data from recent years showed similar breakdowns.

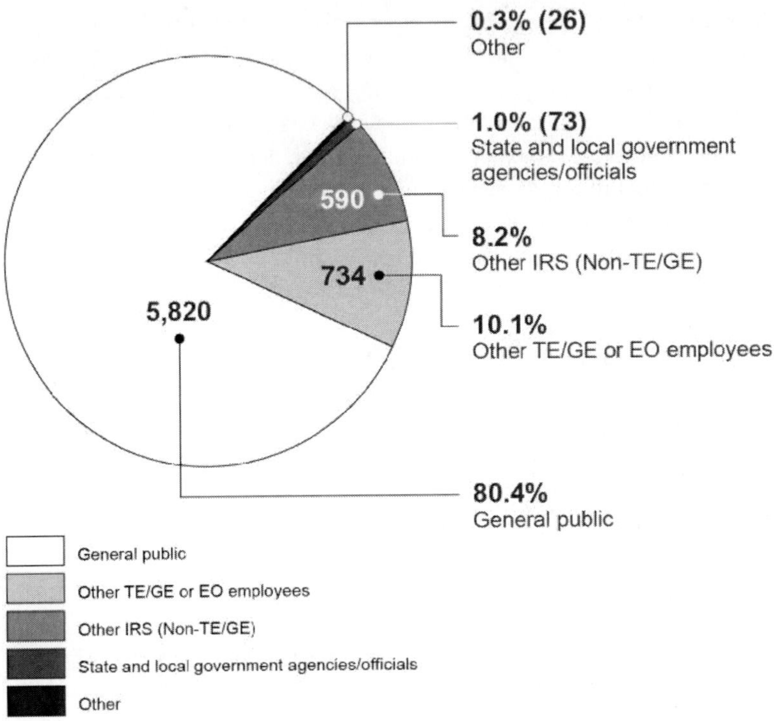

Source: GAO analysis of IRS data. | GAO-15-514.

Note: Data from fiscal years 2012 and 2013 showed similar results, although for both years, referrals from other TE/GE and EO employees were lower, and there were more referrals from "other" sources. Also, there were slightly fewer (about 74 percent of referrals) referrals from the general public in 2012. "Other" includes referrals from news sources, congressional members or staff, and other federal agencies and sources that could be internal or external to TE/GE.

Figure 2. Sources of Exempt Organization Referrals IRS Received in Fiscal Year 2014.

Processing referrals involves several steps, depending on the allegation in the referral or the type of organization involved. Figure 3 summarizes the steps for different referral types.

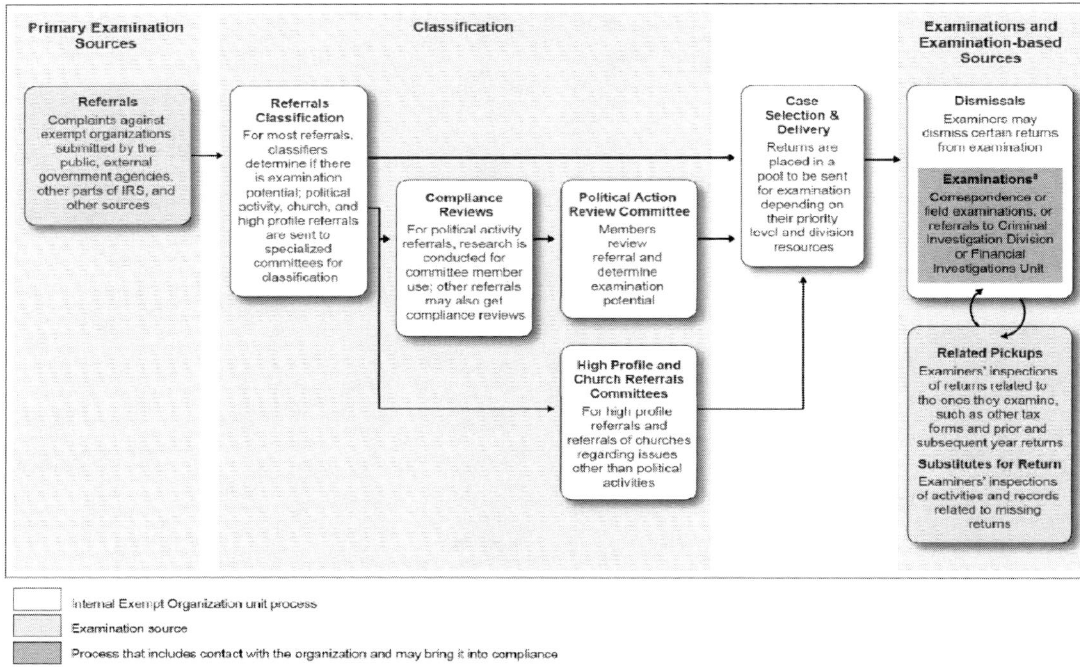

Source: GAO analysis of IRS data. | GAO-15-514.

Notes: Some referrals are filtered out through each of these steps, excepting compliance reviews.

[a]Certain referrals that raise limited concerns are worked as compliance checks rather than examinations.

Figure 3. Exempt Organization Examination Selection Process for Referrals.

Referral classification. EO currently has five classifiers, part of Exempt Organization Examinations, who sort incoming referrals into basic categories, based on an initial review of the referral. All referrals are to be logged into the Referral Database. Referrals are sorted to identify those that do not involve exempt organizations and therefore should go to other IRS divisions (misroutes), referrals that do not mention an organization or a violation of the tax code ("no issue" referrals), and referrals that should be classified for possible examination. After sorting, EO sends an acknowledgment letter to the individual who submitted the referral (except IRS employees).

The Referral Database

The Referral Database houses information on each exempt organization referral, even for referrals that do not go through the full classification process, such as referrals that were mistakenly sent to EO rather than other units, or referrals that do not have enough information to classify. Throughout the classification process, the database is used to log the actions on the referral. Specifically, the database includes

- the classifier's comments;
- codes, which categorize the complaint(s);
- for committee referrals, the comments and decisions for each of the three committee members reviewing the referral;
- the final determination (decision) of whether the referral is selected for examination, not selected for examination, selected for compliance check or compliance review, or transferred to another IRS division; and
- for referrals selected for examination, a priority level.

Source: GAO analysis of IRS guidance. | GAO-15-514

Each of these classifiers specializes in one or more types of referrals, such as political activity referrals, and reviews those referrals for examination potential, according to the EO referrals manager. The majority of referrals are considered general referrals, meaning that a single classifier makes a decision about examination potential. For these referrals, there are no specific criteria for identifying examination potential. Instead, referrals are classified using the facts and circumstances of each referral, which involves a classifier using his or her experience, and all available data on the referral, to determine whether potential noncompliance exists. Some referrals, such as those originating with whistleblowers[24] or those pertaining to the Tax Equity and Fiscal Responsibility Act,[25] have additional steps or criteria for classification. The classifier is responsible for documenting his or her decision in the Referral Database, as well as providing an explanation for the decision. According to the EO referrals manager, this includes mentioning any research conducted to corroborate the allegation and, for referrals classified as "no issue," an explanation of the decision not to pursue.

Referral committees. Referrals that deal with political activity allegations or what IRS has identified as sensitive allegations or organizations are also reviewed by a three person committee.[26] The committees are composed of a rotating set of senior examination staff or managers who make the final decision about examination potential. According to the Internal Revenue Manual (IRM), committee members should rotate every 12 months on a staggered schedule to maintain continuity and expertise; volunteers are to be solicited in a memorandum from the Director of Examination for EO.[27] EO has three types of committees to review referrals.

1) **Political Activities Referral Committee.** Reviews allegations of potentially noncompliant exempt organization political activities, including churches.[28] The Political Activities Referral Committee reviewed 501 referrals in fiscal year 2014.
2) **Church Committee.** Reviews referrals concerning churches for allegations other than political activity.[29] EO currently has two Church Committees, which handle the same types of cases. Church and High Profile Committees (see below) combined reviewed 43 referrals in fiscal year 2014.[30]
3) **High Profile Committee.** Reviews referrals concerning exempt organizations that have attracted media attention, that have financial transactions with known or suspected terrorist organizations, or are referrals from elected officials.

The Reasonable Belief Standard for Referrals

The reasonable belief standard for referrals in the IRM (Part 4, Chapter 75, Section 5.7) states that the requirements are met when "the information item when considered fairly and in light of other reliable information, if available, demonstrates that a violation of the EO tax laws may have occurred or appears likely to lead to the discovery of a violation upon examination. In making this determination, EO Referral Committee members are expected to use their experience, judgment, and concern for fairness."

Source: Internal Revenue Manual. | GAO-15-514

A committee may also review referrals involving other factors, identified by a classifier, which indicate that committee review is desirable for reasons of "fairness and integrity," according to the *Referrals Procedures* document.[31]

Each committee member is responsible for reviewing the referral and providing a determination on examination potential, along with comments, into the Referral Database. Political activity referrals, and other referrals as requested, are sent for a compliance review to provide additional information to committee members to inform their decisions. Referral committee members are to use the reasonable belief standard as criteria for examination selection. The outcome for the referral is determined by a majority, i.e., at least two of the three committee members being in agreement. This outcome is automatically tallied in the database when members enter a decision. Committee decisions are considered final and cannot be overturned, although, as discussed below, church examinations must go through additional steps before initiation.

Referrals prioritization. For each referral selected for potential examination in fiscal year 2014, a priority level was assigned that guides how quickly the referral is sent to the field for examination. For political activity referrals, the Political Activities Referral Committee determines whether a political activity referral is high priority or "other," based on criteria in the *Referrals Procedures* document.[32] All other referrals are assigned one of seven priority levels. For fiscal year 2014, priority levels were intended to feed into 16 workload priorities, as laid out in a memorandum from the Director of EO Examinations.[33] These priorities guided examination management in deciding which cases to work. EO management has discontinued the prioritization memoranda, according to EO officials. Instead, starting with fiscal year 2015, referrals requiring collaboration with another IRS business division and those dealing with fraud are considered high priority, and therefore will be examined before other referrals. The Case Selection and Delivery unit assigns other referrals to the field based on grade level and location of examination staff, as described earlier in this report. Referrals that are assigned for examination may be dismissed if examination management or staff do not find examination potential, if the return is approaching the statute of limitations, or for other reasons.

Referral outcomes. Most referrals are not selected for potential examination; referrals that are selected may not actually become examinations due to resource constraints, or other considerations, according to EO officials. Table 5 summarizes referrals processing during fiscal year 2014.

Table 5. Outcomes for Referrals Processed in Fiscal Year 2014, by Referral Type[a]

	Duplicates[b]	**In process[c]**	**Selected for potential examination**	**Not selected for examination[d]**	**Total**
General	912	1,900	946	3,453	**7,211**
Political Activities Referral Committee	188	281	169	356	**994**
Church or High Profile Committees	338	86	27	444	**895**
Misroutes and uncategorized	4	5	2	923	**934**
Total	**1,442**	**2,272**	**1,144**	**5,176**	**10,034**

Source: GAO analysis of IRS Exempt Organizations Referral Database, as of Sept. 26, 2014.| GAO-15-514.

[a]The table shows all referrals that had processing activity during fiscal year 2014; some referrals were received in previous years.

[b]Duplicates are either a referral on the same organization and issue sent in by multiple people, or the same referral sent in by the same person.

[c]As of the end of the fiscal year, these referrals had not yet completed the classification process.

[d]Referrals not selected for examination include no issue referrals, referrals to be reviewed for possible future examination, and those that were transferred to compliance reviews, compliance checks, or other groups.

Churches Undergo Additional Reviews before Examinations Are Initiated

Statutory requirements must be met before EO can initiate an examination on a church.[34] Specifically, after determining that there is reasonable belief (based on facts and circumstances recorded in writing) that a church may not qualify for exemption, IRS must first issue a *Notice of Inquiry* to the church.[35] An inquiry serves as a basis for determining whether the organization qualifies for exemption as a church, whether it is engaged in activities subject to tax, or whether an excess benefit transaction has occurred.[36] If there is a reasonable belief that an inquiry is necessary—based on facts and circumstances of the case, including committee review if a referral is involved—then the information is sent to a designated official, who must be an "appropriate high-level Treasury official."[37] Currently, the designated official is the Director, Exempt Organizations, who must also get concurrence from the TE/GE Commissioner, according to EO officials. Under the statute, an "appropriate high-level Treasury official" must reasonably believe that an inquiry is necessary.[38]

According to the IRM, division counsel and an EO area manager must review the notice before it can be issued.[39] If a church does not respond to the inquiry or cannot resolve IRS's concerns, EO examination staff will prepare a *Notice of Examination* and a memorandum on why an examination is necessary, according to the IRM.[40] Two levels of division counsel and the designated official must approve the notice. These statutory procedures are followed for employment tax issues, but do not apply to routine requests, such as solicitation of a delinquent employment tax return or information requested to resolve inconsistencies revealed in the matching program, among other things.[41]

EO initiated one examination on a church in fiscal year 2014, and two in fiscal year 2013.[42] EO officials told us they suspended new church examinations from 2009 to January 2013[43] after a 2009 district court case,[44] which ruled that, at the time, the designated official was not the "appropriate high-level Treasury official" envisioned by Congress.[45] In 2009, IRS issued a Notice of Proposed Rulemaking putting forward the Director of EO as the designated (i.e. "appropriate high-level Treasury") official; to date, final regulations have not been issued.[46] EO officials said they resumed church examinations, based on existing regulations, and modified the process by adding another level of review, as the designated official is the Director of EO, who acts in concurrence with the TE/GE Commissioner.[47]

Organizations with Complex Financial Transactions May Be Reviewed for Potential Fraud

The Financial Investigations Unit examines exempt organizations that are selected as a result of projects or queries, or have been identified with potential indicators of fraud. There were 121 Financial Investigations Unit examinations of exempt organizations initiated in fiscal year 2014. Classifiers and examination staff may refer returns to the Financial Investigations Unit if they believe indicators of fraud or other criteria are met, as listed in the IRM.[48] Examination staff who suspect fraud fill out a form describing the issues and consult with an exempt organizations fraud specialist. A Fraud Technical Advisor must approve placing the return in fraud development status. If the Financial Investigations Unit finds indicators of fraud, the case will be referred to IRS's Criminal Investigation division. The Financial Investigations Unit has also provided classifiers with supplemental criteria to help identify potential fraud. Classifiers may also refer a return to the Financial Investigations Unit.

The Criminal Investigation division investigates potential criminal fraud. 49 There were 96 criminal investigations initiated on exempt organizations in fiscal year 2014. Criminal investigations of exempt organizations can originate in one of two ways, according to a senior IRS analyst working in Criminal Investigations.

- **Referrals from EO Examination.** Examination staff may recommend a case if they identify general fraud indicators and the case meets criminal criteria. They will suspend the examination, and Criminal Investigation will review the case. EO Examination makes referrals via a form, which explains the basis for the suspected fraud. Criminal Investigation staff will develop the case, identify any possible charges, and make a recommendation to the U.S. Attorney for prosecution, which may lead to an indictment and eventual trial.

- **Referrals from U.S. Attorneys, local law enforcement, and other informants.** Criminal Investigation staff conduct preliminary reviews of the referral, and then develop cases in the same manner as those originating from EO Examination.

The criteria for moving forward with a prosecution resulting from a referral are based on the judicial district of the taxpayer. Each U.S. Attorney has different types of cases or minimum tax revenue loss they are willing to prosecute; there is no checklist of criteria, according to a senior IRS analyst working in Criminal Investigations. For example, one region may prosecute a tax revenue loss of $250,000, while another region may prosecute a loss of $100,000.

DESIGN AND IMPLEMENTATION OF SOME CONTROLS WAS ADEQUATE; OTHER CONTROLS SHOULD BE STRENGTHENED TO REDUCE THE RISK OF UNFAIR EXAMINATION SELECTION

We found that the design of certain examination selection controls aligned with the IRM or with standards for effective internal control (see sidebar and figure 4). We also found that the implementation of some of these controls (i.e. the steps used for examination selection) aligned with these standards. As such, these controls may serve as tools to help EO meet TE/GE's mission of applying the tax law with integrity and fairness. However, we found that other controls were deficient in either their design or their implementation. These control deficiencies increase the risk that EO could fall short of TE/GE's mission and select organizations for examination in an unfair manner—for example, based on an organization's religious, educational, political, or other views. Effective internal control helps agencies adapt to shifting environments, evolving demands, and new priorities. As programs change and agencies strive to improve operational processes and implement new technology, management should continually evaluate its internal control system so that it is effective and updated when necessary.

What Are Internal Controls and Why Do They Matter?

One way federal agencies can improve accountability in achieving their missions is by implementing an effective internal control system. Internal control is not one event, but rather is a series of actions and activities that occur throughout an entity's operations and on an ongoing basis. Internal controls provide reasonable, not absolute, assurance of meeting agency objectives. Two examples of internal control standards are that an agency should ensure that significant events are clearly documented, and that key duties should be divided among different people. For more information on internal control standards, see the Green Book, GAO/AIMD-00-21.3.1, *Standards for Internal Control in the Federal Government* (November 1999, Washington, D.C.). A newer version of the Green Book, GAO-14-704G, *Standards for Internal Control in the Federal Government* (September 2014, Washington, D.C.), goes into effect in fiscal year 2016.

Source: GAO. | GAO-15-514

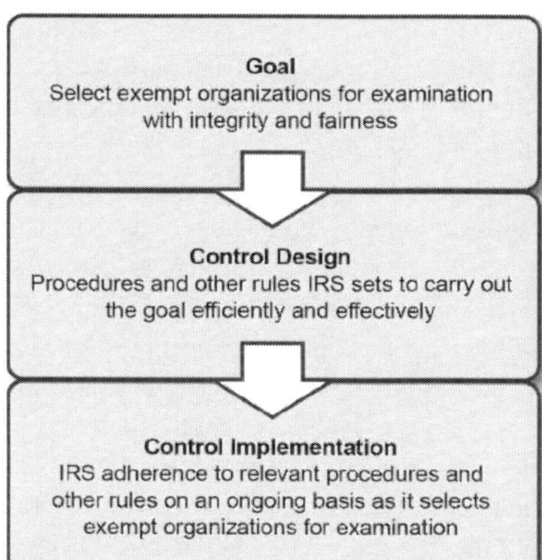

Source: GAO. | GAO-15-514

Figure 4. Using Internal Controls in Selecting Exempt Organizations for Examination.

Multiple Examination Selection Processes Met Both Design and Implementation Control Standards

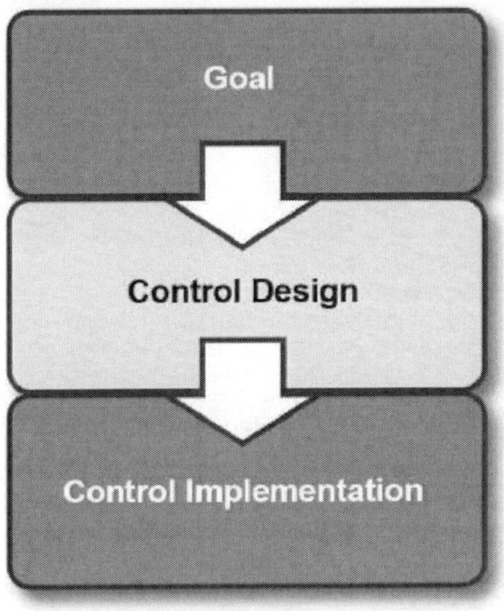

Source: GAO. | GAO-15-514

We found several examples of examination selection processes that met design and implementation internal control standards.

Design of Internal Controls. Agency management designs control activities in response to its objectives and risks to achieve an effective internal control system. Control activities are the policies, procedures, techniques, and mechanisms that enforce management directives to achieve an agency's objectives and address related risks. Internal control standards require control activities to be effective and efficient in accomplishing an agency's control objective. As part of their control activities, agencies must ensure that internal controls are clearly documented. IRS requires primary sources of guidance with an IRS-wide or division-wide impact—such as policy documents, procedures, and guidelines—to be included in the IRM.[50] This requirement is intended to ensure that IRS employees have the approved policy and guidance they need to carry out their responsibilities in administering the tax laws.

Internal Control Standard: Establish Effective and Efficient Control Activities.

Establish control activities, to include ensuring that internal controls are clearly documented.

Source: GAO. | GAO-15-514

In alignment with IRM requirements, EO maintains well-documented procedures for several examination selection processes. For example, EO management has developed IRM sections for referrals classification, claims processing, Financial Investigations Unit case processing, and examinations. During our focus groups, employees working closely with these IRM procedures generally reported they were useful.[51] For examinations, there were IRM sections on several different types of examinations and steps in the process, including substitutes for return, related pickups, the Team Examination Program (used for large and complex organizations), and church examinations.

In focus groups, we found that staff who use these (and other IRM sections) to conduct their work generally view them as valuable tools that help them administer the tax law (see text box).

Selected EO employee focus group participants' statements regarding IRM procedures:

"I came off the streets and can read the IRM and understand it. Kudos to the IRM to the degree that this is my springboard to know what to do and how to do it."

"The IRM is excellent, it tells you everything."

"I go straight to the IRM. It's there to provide fair and consistent treatment."

To further align with IRM requirements, EO is working to draft and implement IRM procedures for testing and adopting 990 analytics queries.[52] For example, EO will likely formalize its current practice of requiring approval to test queries not already listed in EO's annual workplan, according to one of the draft IRM sections. This new draft IRM also describes certain development work to be conducted prior to implementing a query. EO plans for both IRMs to be implemented in the last quarter of this fiscal year, according to EO officials. Having written procedures will help ensure that EO is taking action to address internal control risks. EO's publishing these procedures in the IRM increases transparency to the public.

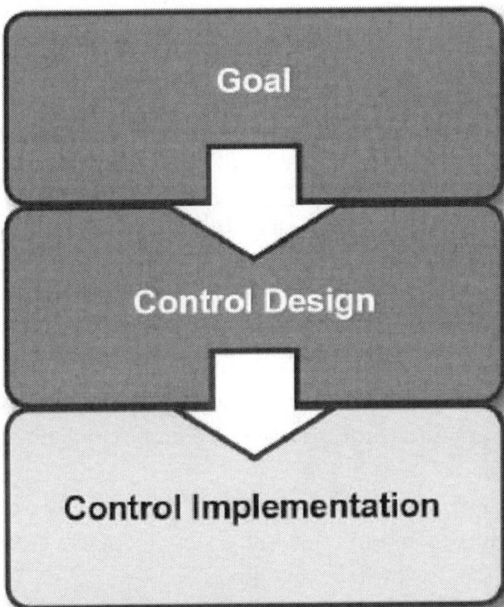

Source: GAO. | GAO-15-514

Implementation of Internal Controls. Internal control standards require that control design be adhered to in practice, known as control implementation. EO's control design for examination selection includes requirements for various types of documentation of examination decisions and approvals. We found that multiple EO processes successfully implemented several types of such controls. For example, both EOCA procedures and referrals procedures require Case Chronology Records— records that track actions taken on a case—and we found that in practice, 100 percent of cases closed in fiscal year 2014 contained Case Chronology Records.[53] See appendix II for more examples of successful implementation of controls for recording decisions and approvals.

Internal Control Standard: Establish a Positive Control Environment.

Management and employees should establish and maintain an environment throughout the organization that sets a positive and supportive attitude toward internal control and conscientious management. Several key factors affect the control environment, including integrity and ethical values maintained and demonstrated by staff.

Source: GAO. | GAO-15-514

EO Has Established Key Factor for Building a Positive Control Environment

Internal control standards require that management and employees establish and maintain an organization-wide environment that sets a positive and supportive attitude toward internal control and conscientious management. An agency's management plays a key role in providing leadership in this area, especially in setting guidance for proper behavior. The IRM sets standards of conduct for treating taxpayers fairly, stating that it is the duty of agency officials to determine the correct amount of tax owed with strict impartiality as between the government and taxpayer, and without favoritism or discrimination between taxpayers.[54] It also says that agency representatives must adhere to the law and recognized standards of legal construction in making conclusions of fact or application of the law.[55] We found in focus groups that EO employees who conduct examinations and other reviews consistently equated fairness with assessing organizations strictly by whether they comply with tax law and with treating similar types of taxpayers equally. EO employees' relatively uniform understanding of fairness and the alignment of their understanding with the IRM is a significant step toward EO achieving a positive control environment, the foundation for all other control standards.

Selected EO employee focus group participants' statements regarding the meaning of fairness:

"(You should) treat everyone alike, it doesn't matter who filed the information, it's what they filed. (You look to see) are they doing the right activity (as permitted by their tax exempt status), organizing properly, and capturing transactions accurately. It doesn't matter the perspective of an organization. And you should support everything you do by regulations and code."

"You should treat each organization in a specific regulation section in the same manner. If it's a 501(c)(4), if one organization is allowed to do something, then they all are—they are treated fairly and equally."

Other Controls Needed Improvement or Standards Were Not Followed

We found that while EO had established various procedures over its examination selection processes, there were several areas where EO's controls were not well designed or implemented (see table 6). Taken as a whole, these control deficiencies increase the risk that EO could select organizations for examination in an unfair manner—for example, based on an organization's religious, educational, political, or other views.

Table 6. Summary of Identified Internal Control Deficiencies by Examination Selection Process

	Identified deficiency	Affected process(es)
Control Design	Procedures not documented in IRM	Compliance checks Compliance reviews EOCA classification
	Some outdated or inaccurate aspects of procedures	Referrals Dismissed examinations Team Examination Program[a]
	Insufficient monitoring requirements for case approvals and explanations	EOCA classification Dismissed examinations Examinations (Claims) Referrals[b]
	Inadequate IRS process for tracking and maintaining closed case files	Examinations[c]

	Identified deficiency	Affected process(es)
	Some inadequate documentation of project selection criteria and controls for certain project activities	Form 990 data analytics Ongoing programs Projects
Control Implementation	Lack of data dictionaries for databases	Compliance checks Compliance reviews EOCA classification Examinations Referrals
	Lack of Privacy Impact Assessments for databases	Compliance checks Compliance reviews EOCA classification Referrals
	Only one classifier is reviewing each type of referral	Referrals
	Referral committee members are not rotating	Referrals

Source: GAO analysis. | GAO-15-514

NOTES:

[a]The Team Examination Program conducts examinations on large and complex organizations.

[b]The results of our review were statistically indeterminate, but of potential concern.

[c]Claims and related pickup files.

Deficiencies in Control Design

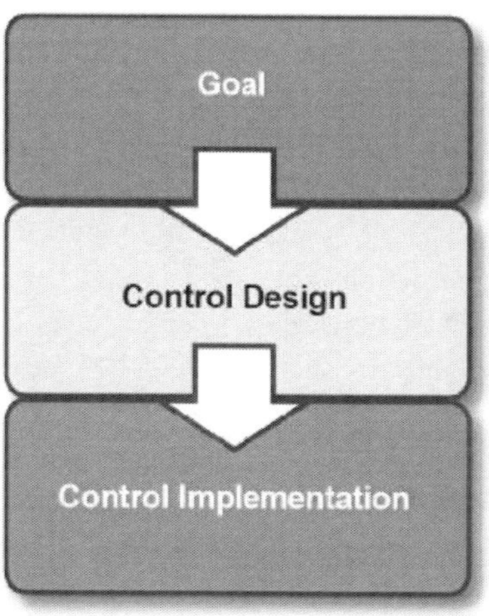

Source: GAO. | GAO-15-514

Compliance Check, Compliance Review, and EOCA Classification Procedures Are Not Documented in the IRM as Required

Internal control standards require that controls, and an agency's documentation of them, should be properly managed and maintained. As noted previously, IRS requires primary sources of guidance with an IRS-wide or organizational impact—such as policy documents, procedures, and guidelines—to be included in the IRM.[56] This requirement is intended to ensure that IRS employees have the approved policy and guidance they need to carry out their responsibilities in administering the tax laws. Moreover, including primary guidance in the IRM fulfills certain legal requirements. For example, one way IRS complies with the Freedom of Information Act is by making most IRM guidance available online to the public.[57]

Internal Control Standard: Properly Manage and Maintain Documentation.

Controls and an agency's documentation of them should be properly managed and maintained.

Source: GAO. | GAO-15-514

EO's primary sources of guidance for compliance checks, compliance reviews, and EOCA classification are not included in the IRM, as required by the IRM. In 2008, EO officials drafted high-level descriptions of compliance checks and compliance reviews for the IRM, but these were never published. According to EO officials, staffing levels were insufficient to complete this work. Instead, EO has developed procedure documents for compliance checks, compliance reviews, and EOCA classification outside of the IRM. These documents provide instructions to staff about the required approvals, documentation, and other steps taken as part of each case selection process. The compliance check and compliance review processes also have job aid documents with information relevant to processing cases.

By not complying with agency requirements and standards for internal control, the internal procedures for compliance checks, compliance reviews, and EOCA classification are not covered by the same standards as the IRM. For example, deviations from the IRM are only allowed with approval by executive management and with appropriate communication to employees, whereas these standards do not explicitly apply to other documents. Reliance on procedures that are outside of the IRM creates the risk that EO staff could deviate from procedures without executive management approval, which could result in unfair selection of organizations' returns for examination. Excluding these procedures from the IRM also reduces transparency, since they would be available to the public if they were in the IRM.

Some Aspects of Procedures for Examination Selection Are Outdated or Inaccurate

Internal Control Standard: Document Internal Controls.

Controls should be documented and properly managed and maintained.

Source: GAO. | GAO-15-514

Internal control standards require that controls should be documented and properly managed and maintained. According to the IRM, IRS program managers are responsible for ensuring that IRM content is reviewed annually for accuracy and completeness and for analyzing issues that may necessitate changes.[58] Likewise, supplemental guidance—such as job aids and desk guides—must be reviewed at least annually to ensure the content remains accurate.[59] We found that EO examination selection procedures, including the IRM, contained outdated and, in some cases, inaccurate material, such as the following examples:

- A provision in the IRM for manually selecting returns for the Team Examination Program, rather than using standardized criteria based on an organization's income and assets, is not actually used, according to EO officials.[60] Further, the IRM requires that a worksheet be completed for returns under consideration for the program. The worksheet includes a section on factors considered in the examination selection decision and a section for reviews and signatures. EO officials stated that the worksheet has not been used since 2012 and they are currently updating that section of the IRM.
- A section on closing dismissed examinations requires that a stamp with management signatures be placed on original, non-electronic,

returns that are dismissed.[61] However, this requirement is not implemented consistently—in our file review, we found very few of the paper files had this stamp—and given the increasing reliance on electronic copies of returns, this requirement may be becoming less relevant. Further, EO has another control in place (discussed in appendix II) which suffices to document management approval for dismissed returns. EO management said they will use the signatures on paper returns until all forms can be electronically signed.

- A section on requirements for opening an examination of a related return states that staff should document the manager's approval to expand the examination, and a written statement of approval should be included in the examination file.[62] EO officials told us that managers approve related pick-ups within the Reporting Compliance Case Management System (RCCMS), the database EO uses for tracking examinations, which has replaced the need for written documentation of approval within the file.[63]

We also found examples of outdated and inaccurate guidance in procedures documents. Specifically, in the September 2014 *Referrals Procedures* document we found the following:

- The procedures include criteria for sending a referral to a "High Priority Committee." However, there is no High Priority Committee, according to EO officials. The EO officials described this as a "typo" and said that all mentions of the High Priority Committee should be replaced with "High Profile Committee." This mistake was also in the previous year's version of the document.
- The procedures include a requirement that subject matter experts periodically review referrals screened out by the classifier responsible for political activity referrals to confirm that exclusion from committee review is appropriate. EO officials stated that this requirement was originally formulated in 2012, but the reviews have not been conducted because of a subsequent decision to send all political activity referrals for committee review.

We provided EO with these, and other, citations of outdated or inaccurate procedures. The EO Director acknowledged that there are outdated procedures and IRM sections for EO processes, and that many of these are the result of changes that have occurred over the past 18 months. EO officials said they were in the midst of an effort to update outdated and inaccurate guidance in the IRM and anticipated completing this process by the end of August 2015. Outdated and inaccurate procedures pose the risk that employees might follow incorrect procedures and therefore inconsistently administer tax laws.

Monitoring to Ensure Case Files Procedures Were Followed Is Not Sufficient

Internal Control Standard: Conduct Continuous Monitoring.

Conduct monitoring to assess quality over time. Monitoring activities should be continuous and built in, effected by people, and conducted during the course of normal operations.

Source: GAO. | GAO-15-514

According to internal control standards, controls should generally be designed to assure that ongoing monitoring occurs in the course of normal operations. Monitoring involves management assessments of the design and operating effectiveness of internal control systems. It also includes ensuring that individual managers and supervisors know their responsibilities for internal control and the need to make control and control monitoring part of their regular operating processes. We found several deficiencies in closed examination and dismissed examination files, as well as the Referrals, EOCA, and EOCA Classification database files that did not follow procedures. For example, 4 out of 15 committee referrals (political activities, churches, and high profile committees) we reviewed that were selected for examination were missing a required description of the allegation for the committee. Also, an estimated 22 percent of examination returns that were dismissed in fiscal year 2014 did not have the required management signature.[64] Taken as a whole, the deficiencies we found point to insufficient monitoring of case processing. See appendix II for details on the deficiencies.

For each of the processes above, EO provided information on its monitoring activities to help ensure that procedures were followed and that internal controls were operating effectively (see examples in table 7).

Table 7. Examples of EO Monitoring of Examination Selection Processes

Process	Monitoring activities
Referrals	•The EO referrals manager said that he randomly reviews one referral per month from each of the five classifiers, and documents the results. •By having multiple reviewers assess certain referrals, the referrals committees also play a role in ensuring examination selection criteria are applied appropriately.
Compliance checks	•The EOCA manager said that an analyst conducts quality reviews of a random sample of compliance checks, although these are not conducted regularly due to limited resources. A review of the EOCA database showed that out of 61 quality reviews performed for fiscal year 2014, 30 were performed in the approximately 3-month period between February 3 and May 9, 2014, and 24 were performed in the month-and-a-half period between June 30 and August 11, 2014. Seven reviews were performed in the remaining 7-and-a-half months of the fiscal year.
Examinations	•For claims that are dismissed and approved within the Case Selection and Delivery group,the manager said she conducts a review for the required forms and of claim dollar amounts to ensure the correct claim amount is in RCCMS. •EO has procedures that require mandatory reviews of certain examinations, such as those of church tax audits and revocations, to ensure technical and procedural accuracy. EO also has procedures for conducting quality reviews on a sample of cases to evaluate the managerial, technical, and procedural aspects of examination cases. While these reviews span many issues, many unrelated to examination selection processes, certain procedural issues related to examination selection may be assessed, suchas whether prior year, subsequent year, or related returns were included in the examination where warranted.

Source: GAO interviews with EO managers and analysis of EO documentation. | GAO-15-514

In spite of these monitoring activities, we found that EO employees were not always following documentation requirements for select EO examination selection procedures. As such, the current level of ongoing monitoring of examination and database files to ensure that selection decisions are documented and approved, to help ensure fairness, is inadequate. Additional monitoring may help management further evaluate EO's internal control system and make changes to ensure staff are consistently following procedures.

IRS's Process for Tracking and Maintaining Closed Case Files is Inadequate

Internal Control Standard: Properly Manage Documents.

Files should be readily available for review and properly managed and maintained.

Source: GAO. | GAO-15-514

Internal control standards require that files be readily available for review and properly managed and maintained.[65] The IRM also states that all records are required to be efficiently managed until final disposition.[66] Yet IRS was not able to locate all of the examination files we requested for review in a timely way.[67] Based on our estimates, 13 percent[68] of the closed examination files could not be located in time for us to review them during the audit. Specifically, IRS could not locate the files until June 2015, whereas we submitted our original request for the files in early February 2015.

Initially EO officials said the IRS unit that stores the files was unable to locate some of the files. More specifically, EO was told that the unit was unable to locate 3 of 13 of these files' blocks—group of files with consecutive control numbers. This can mean that the block was not created or it was shelved in the wrong location. Other files showed as checked out by IRS staff and not returned to their proper file location. At the end of our audit, IRS located 10 of the missing files after undertaking a specific search for the files. However, the length of time it took to locate these files—nearly 4 months—shows that IRS's process does not ensure that all files are readily available for review.

According to EO officials, missing claims files are generally due to the difficulties of working with paper files. Missing case files can result in lost revenue to the federal government (if a case goes to court), create unnecessary taxpayer burden (if EO later needs to contact the taxpayer regarding material that would have been in the file), make cases unavailable for other units such as quality review groups or advisory groups, and hinder congressional oversight.

EO Lacked Clearly Documented Selection Criteria for Some Projects and Controls for Certain Project Activities

> **Internal Control Standard: Document Internal Controls and Other Significant Events.**
>
> Internal controls and all transactions and significant events need to be clearly documented, and all documentation and records should be properly managed and maintained.
>
> Source: GAO. | GAO-15-514

Internal control standards require that internal controls and all transactions and significant events need to be clearly documented, and that all documentation and records should be properly managed and maintained. EO projects must adhere to certain requirements as they are developed, and these requirements can vary depending on the type of project.[69] All project teams are required to develop project-specific procedures. For projects not associated with Form 990 analytics queries, project teams are required to obtain managerial approval of a proposal. The project proposal should contain, among other things, a description of the project objectives, the criteria to be used to select returns, and the signatures of EO executives and select functional directors. Other requirements depend on whether the cases selected for review are sent directly for field examination, or whether the cases are subject to an intermediate step like a compliance check or compliance review, or an examination through the office/correspondence examination program.[70] The documents associated with a project—such as the proposal, procedures, selection criteria, and training materials—are maintained by the project team leader.

We identified select areas where project documentation could be improved. Our review of 11 project files found that some project requirements were not always met: [71]

- For one project in our sample, EO officials were unable to provide any documentation to support the project requirements we assessed in our project file review, including an approved project proposal.[72]

- Of the seven projects requiring a project proposal—specifically, those projects not associated with 990 analytics queries—we found that none of the project proposals fully described the criteria to be used for the project, including the one project missing documentation. For example, three project proposals described that a judgmental (non-probability) sample would be used but the judgmental sample was not fully described.[73] One of these projects' proposals listed criteria for its first phase, conducted several years ago, but did not reflect selection criteria for a subsequent phase of the project. There was a memorandum in the file describing selection criteria for the more recent phase, but no documented management approval. Another project proposal described how the original sample of cases for which compliance reviews would be conducted was to be pulled, but not how information gathered during the compliance reviews would be used to select cases for examination. EO officials told us that when criteria are added or changed for a project, executives may be briefed and any briefing documents should be included in the project file. However, of the seven projects with incomplete criteria, we only found one file with an executive briefing document describing selection criteria. Two other projects had memoranda in the file describing selection criteria but lacked evidence of executive review or approval.

EO officials told us about improvements they had made to project controls over the past few years. For example, EO officials told us that over the past year they increased efforts to reorganize how project file documentation is stored to help ensure consistency across projects. Likewise, projects using a compliance review or using the office/correspondence examination program had an added control developed toward the end of fiscal year 2013—a document capturing the date on which certain control activities were performed and the individual responsible for each activity.[74] Yet these and other improvements do not address the need to fully describe selection criteria in a project proposal, or document executive briefings and approvals when criteria are added or changed. With project proposals lacking clear selection criteria, EO management risks the potential of projects selecting organizations for review in an unfair manner.

Internal Control Standard: Establish Control Activities To Enforce Management Directives.

Procedures that enforce management directives help ensure that management directives are carried out.

Source: GAO. | GAO-15-514

According to internal control standards, procedures that enforce management directives help ensure that management directives are carried out. Yet EO does not have procedures describing the steps or requirements for triage teams—project team members responsible for deciding which organizations will be examined—when making or documenting examination selection decisions in the project files.[75] Specifically, there is no procedure requiring that triage teams document the specific selection criteria they use to identify organizations for examination. While broad selection criteria are generally described in the project proposal, the triage team may apply additional criteria to filter out cases and align with available resources for working examinations. EO officials told us that these selection criteria decisions would generally be documented in meeting minutes or elsewhere in the project files. Of the two projects using triage teams with closed examinations in fiscal year 2014, one project had dozens of files in the meeting minutes project folder, making it difficult to assess documentation of selection criteria, while the other project was missing documentation altogether.

Similarly, no written procedures exist to ensure that specific triage team examination decisions are documented in the project files. EOCA project procedures require that EOCA staff document triage team examination selection decisions in the EOCA database, but we found that this step did not always occur, and EO officials agreed that our assessment was accurate. EO officials also said that decisions should be documented by triage teams within the project files, which would help ensure that selection decisions at the project-level were readily available for review. Of the two projects using triage teams with closed examinations in fiscal year 2014, the same project as mentioned above was missing project file documentation altogether. The other project had several spreadsheets that tracked examination selection decisions, but it was not always clear which organizations had been selected. More than 2,000 of the compliance checks and compliance reviews conducted in fiscal year 2014 were, or will be, subject to triage team review. Having procedures to ensure triage teams documenting selection criteria and decisions clearly and consistently will help EO ensure that management directives are consistently followed and that examination selection decisions are made fairly.

Internal Control Standard: Record and Communicate Information To Management.

Program managers need operational data to determine whether they are meeting their agencies' strategic and annual performance plans and meeting their goals for accountability for effective and efficient use of resources.

Source: GAO. | GAO-15-514

Internal control standards also state that program managers need operational data to determine whether they are meeting their agencies' strategic and annual performance plans and meeting their goals for accountability for effective and efficient use of resources. We did not review the project files for 2 of the 13 projects in our sample because EO officials told us that these projects were not active in fiscal year 2014. Although no examinations should have been conducted as part of these older projects, we found 156 closed examinations attributed to them in the Returns Inventory and Classification System (RICS) database.[76] For one project, EO officials said that the majority of the project work was conducted between 2006 and 2008 and that the project was concluded by 2009. EO officials said it was likely that EO examination staff miscoded these examinations, and that this is more likely to happen when an examination is associated with a newer project of a similar name. EO uses data on closed examinations, by project, to track performance against workplan goals. Without adequate controls to ensure that examinations are appropriately coded—for example, by ensuring that project codes for closed projects without anticipated future examinations are not utilized by staff—EO management may not have the information it needs to ensure the efficient and effective use of resources.

Deficiencies in Control Implementation

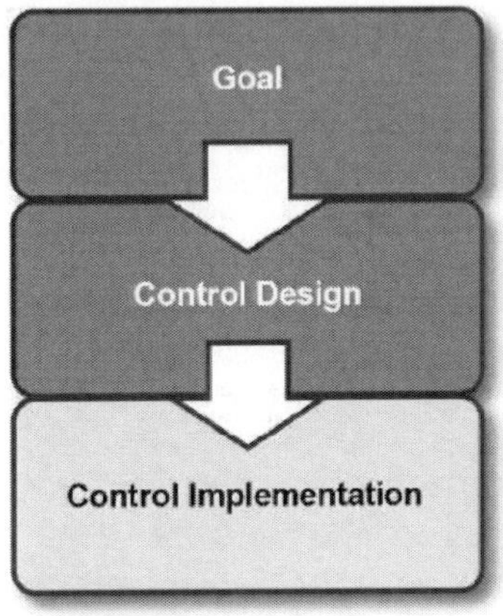

Source: GAO. | GAO-15-514

EO Lacks Complete Data Dictionaries for Examination Selection Databases

The IRM states that all data elements in IRS databases should be defined and documented as part of the database design process.[77] However, EO does not have complete and up-to-date data dictionaries—documents that define each data element in an information system—for the systems it uses to track and document examination selection decisions. EO does not have a data dictionary for the Reporting Compliance Case Management System (RCCMS)—which EO uses for tracking examinations and will use for additional selection purposes in the future— nor for the EOCA or EOCA classification databases.[78] EO's data dictionary for the referrals database is incomplete, as it defines fewer than half of the data elements in the database. In addition, EO has an outdated data dictionary for RICS, which it uses to identify populations of cases for review.[79] For all of these systems, EO describes selected data elements and how they are to be used in procedure, training, or other documents. For example, EOCA procedure and job aid documents define several codes used in the EOCA database and define common data elements from the database.

EO officials cited various reasons for not having data dictionaries or for having outdated dictionaries. For RCCMS, EO officials said they use as their data dictionary a document which lists the data elements within each data table. The document shows the relationships between data elements, but does not contain a description of each data element. Officials overseeing the EOCA and EOCA classification databases said they did not have adequate resources to develop this type of documentation, and also that data elements are already defined in other documents.[80] The manager overseeing the referrals database said that the database predates his tenure, but fields have been added over the years, particularly in response to audits conducted by the Treasury Inspector General of Tax Administration. Finally, EO officials said the RICS data dictionary is outdated due to lack of staffing and because documents listing transcribed lines from Form 990 filings, which are used by staff to develop examination selection queries, were kept up to date instead.

Without complete and up-to-date data dictionaries, data element definitions are not available in a single document for individuals newly using the system, including EO employees and system developers. Also, since data dictionaries assist users and developers with understanding these databases, not having an adequate and up-to-date dictionary may result in an increased risk of data elements not being used accurately. To illustrate, the referrals database has certain obsolete data elements used to document decisions when procedures were different, yet we found that individuals were sometimes still entering information into these fields.

EO Lacks Required Privacy Impact Assessments for Some Examination Selection Databases

The E-Government Act of 2002 requires agencies to conduct a Privacy Impact Assessment before developing or procuring information technology systems or projects that collect, maintain, or disseminate information about members of the public or initiating a new electronic collection of information for 10 or more persons.[81] EO has not conducted Privacy Impact Assessments for three of its databases used in examination selection processes—specifically, the referrals, EOCA, and EOCA classification databases.[82] These systems house thousands of records describing reviews conducted on exempt organizations, including organizations' names, Employer Identification Numbers, and other taxpayer information.

We were initially told that the Tax Exempt and Government Entities (TE/GE) division does not consider the databases to be systems, and therefore they were not covered by requirements in the E-Government Act. However, in responding to our subsequent questions on the subject, IRS Chief Counsel stated that these databases likely fall within the purview of the Act. Accordingly, in early April, EO officials began to evaluate whether the databases require a Privacy Impact Assessment with IRS's Office of Privacy,

Governmental Liaison, and Disclosure (henceforth, the Privacy Office). This evaluation involved TE/GE responding to a questionnaire and the Privacy Office assessing these responses to determine whether Privacy Impact Assessments are necessary to comply with E-Government Act requirements. 83 As a result of the assessment, the Privacy Office determined that Privacy Impact Assessments were required for each of these three systems. According to a Privacy Office official, creating a final approved Privacy Impact Assessment can take 1 to 3 months.

Only One Classifier Reviews Each Type of Referral, Risking Potential Perception of Unfairness and Succession Planning Problems

Internal Control Standard: Segregate Duties.

Key duties and responsibilities need to be divided or segregated among different people to reduce the risk of error.

Source: GAO. | GAO-15-514

Internal control standards require that key duties and responsibilities be divided or segregated among different people to reduce the risk of error and to achieve organizational goals. Referrals classification divides work among its five classifiers based on expertise for a particular type of referral. One classifier is responsible for each of the following area(s):

1) Fraud and terrorism referrals, and referrals that request collaboration with another IRS division.
2) Political activity referrals.
3) Tax Equity and Fiscal Responsibility Act and state referrals.
4) Employee status,[84] whistleblower, and international referrals.
5) High profile and church committee referrals.

In addition, each classifier, except for the individual responsible for political activity referrals, also reviews general referrals, which are referrals that do not fit into these categories.[85] The classifiers review the referrals they are responsible for and make classification determinations. Each classifier has several years of experience and some have received specialized training to work with the types of referrals under his or her specialty. Aside from general referrals, classifiers are not cross-trained on referral specialties, according to the EO referrals manager.

Internal Control Standard: Effectively Manage Human Capital.

Management should ensure that skill needs are continually assessed and that the organization is able to obtain a workforce that has the required skills that match those necessary to achieve organizational goals.

Source: GAO. | GAO-15-514

The specialization of the classifiers allows for in-depth knowledge of complex issues and for the opportunity to apply experience; however, internal control risks accompany this approach. First, for political activity, church, and high profile referrals, the classifier appears to serve as an initial gatekeeper for determining whether a referral is reviewed by a committee. Although committee reviews are intended as a safeguard against unfairness in the examination selection process, referrals that do not make it past the classifier do not undergo committee review. For example, according to the EO referrals manager, all political activity referrals are supposed to go to the Political Activities Referral Committee to ensure that they receive the benefits of committee review. However, the political activity referrals classifier exercises some judgment in determining which referrals are categorized as political activity referrals. Further, in our review of the Referrals Database, we found that about 5 percent of political activity referrals classified in fiscal year 2014 were not reviewed by the committee. The classifier for the high profile and church referrals has more discretion in deciding which referrals go to the committee. In our database review, we found that about 91 percent of these referrals were not reviewed by the committee. According to the EO referrals manager, this is often because they did not contain enough information or did not deal with tax issues (known as "no issue" referrals).[86] These numbers highlight the extent to which classifiers make decisions outside of the committee review process.

According to internal control standards, key duties and responsibilities should be divided or segregated among different people to reduce the risk of error. Spreading classification responsibilities for sensitive referrals to more than one classifier could help decrease the potential influence of any one classifier. Even if other safeguards are in place, having the same individual initially classify all political activity or all high profile and church referrals creates the potential for unfairness, particularly for referrals that the classifier labels as "no issue" and therefore are not sent for committee review.

The lack of cross-training among the classifiers also creates concerns about succession planning. For example, three of the five classifiers are eligible for retirement, according to the EO referrals manager. Internal control standards require that management should ensure that skill needs are continually assessed and that the organization is able to obtain a workforce that has the required skills that match those necessary to achieve organizational goals. As a part of its human capital planning, management should also consider how best to retain valuable employees, plan for their eventual succession, and ensure continuity of needed skills and abilities. The EO referrals manager agreed that they should have a succession plan, but said that they are working with a "bare bones" staff and do not have the resources to take time away from current classifiers' duties for training. TE/GE executives agreed that cross-training classifiers is ideal, but also stated that it is currently not feasible given existing resources. However, without cross-training or provisions for succession planning, EO is risking its ability to process referrals upon the departure of one of its classifiers. It is inevitable that classifiers will eventually need to be replaced. By completing some cross-training ahead of those departures, referrals classification could benefit from overlapping specialties and spreading responsibility for classifying sensitive referrals to reduce the potential for error and potential unfairness.

Referral Committee Membership is Not Rotating as Required

Internal Control Standard: Establish Control Activities To Enforce Management Directives.

Procedures that enforce management directives help ensure that management directives are carried out.

Source: GAO. | GAO-15-514

According to internal control standards, procedures that enforce management directives, such as IRM requirements on the rotation of staff, help ensure that management directives are carried out. Management should also design and implement internal controls based on the related costs and benefits. The IRM requires that committee members rotate every 12 months, on a staggered schedule.[87]

The members of the referral review committees are not rotating every 12 months. Based on start dates for committee members provided by EO and our database review, we found 87 percent of current committee members were serving for more than a 12 month period, as of April 30, 2015.[88] Specifically, current committee members who exceeded their 12- month tenures have been serving on the committees for an average of 34 months (see table 8). In addition, although not reflected in this table, some committee members may have served on another committee prior to their current term, according to the EO referrals manager. Our database review showed that some committee members have served on committees since 2009.

Table 8. Number of Months Served by Current Referrals Committee Members, as of April 30, 2015

			Committees		
	High Profile	Political Activity	Political Activity	Churches	Churches
Member 1	39	34	34	40	34
Member 2	25	34	34	40	34
Member 3	28	7	20	40	9

Source: IRS officials. | GAO-15-514

NOTE: The second political activity committee listed here is primarily responsible for reviewing returns identified through data analytics queries. However, when workload is high for the Political Activities Referral Committee, the second committee reviews referrals, according to the EO referrals manager.

Rotating staff may help ensure that a variety of staff serve on the committees, which serve as a safeguard in the classification of political activity and sensitive referrals. If the required committee rotation serves as an internal control to address risks in the referrals examination selection process, then by not following its procedures, EO has the potential to fall short of its goal of fairness.

Committee member volunteers are to be senior EO technical employees, and should be solicited in an annual memorandum from the Director of EO Examinations, according to the IRM.[89] EO did not have records of an issued memorandum soliciting volunteers, although all of the current members are volunteers, according to an EO official.[90] The EO referrals manager told us that it is difficult to get volunteers because of the potentially high volume of work, particularly for political activity referrals, and the difficulty providing prospective committee members with an estimate of the time commitment required. However, by not utilizing all avenues for soliciting volunteers—such as the memorandum from the Director of EO Examinations—EO is not reaching the pool of potential volunteers and maximizing opportunities to rotate committee members.

Yet management should also design and implement internal controls based on the related costs and benefits. The current committee members have likely developed an expertise in assessing these cases, and training new members may require additional resources. Although a provision for rotations is consistent with internal controls, it is possible that a rotation of more than 12 months may suffice. If EO believes that to be the case, it could revise the IRM accordingly.

CONCLUSION

The Exempt Organizations unit (EO) is faced with the challenging task of overseeing the diverse population of exempt organizations and enforcing their compliance with the tax laws. EO's reliance on a variety of sources and processes to select organizations' returns for examination underscores the importance of it having a robust internal control system to ensure selection fairness and integrity, in accordance with the Tax Exempt and Government Entities (TE/GE) division's mission. EO has some controls in place that are consistent with internal control standards, and has implemented some of these controls successfully. However, there are several areas where EO's control system could be strengthened, as noted by the control deficiencies identified in this report. Many of these deficiencies pose a risk that could lead to returns being selected, or not selected, for examination based on criteria or practices that fall short of TE/GE's mission of ensuring fairness and integrity. For example, internal controls monitoring is one way to help reduce risk, but without consistent monitoring, there is the possibility returns could be selected for unfair reasons.

Control design improvements. To reduce the risk of returns being selected unfairly, EO could make several improvements to its examination selection control design. Formalizing additional procedures in the Internal Revenue Manual (IRM) would ensure coverage using standards that dictate when deviations from selection procedures are appropriate, and would increase transparency. Ensuring that all procedures are current and accurate would reduce the risk of employees following incorrect procedures and administering tax laws inconsistently. Enhancing both the monitoring of database files used to document examination selection decisions and monitoring the content of examination files would increase EO management's ability to address and rectify problems such as missing signatures, errors in applying criteria, and inappropriate justifications for case selection or dismissals—each of which might result in case selection decisions inconsistent with TE/GE's mission. Improving tracking of closed examination files would have multiple benefits, including facilitating congressional oversight. More consistent documentation and approval of criteria in EO's project files would reduce the risk that inappropriate selection criteria could be developed. Finally, more accurate coding of examinations would reduce the risk of ineffective or inefficient resource allocation decisions for compliance activities.

Control implementation improvements. EO could also make several improvements to control implementation that would reduce the risk of returns being selected unfairly. Maintaining up-to-date EO database documentation of data element definitions used to track case selection would reduce the risk of inaccurate use of data elements. Additionally, EO has the opportunity to provide cross-training for referrals classifiers and to quickly benefit from their resulting skills enhancements. This would allow shared responsibility for reviewing political activity and sensitive referrals, and also could reduce the potential for unfairness. Providing training for classifiers currently onboard, rather than waiting until a classifier departs and it becomes a necessity, would help preempt a significant void of knowledge and an increased backlog of work. Finally, rotating the staff who serve on referral review committees would help ensure that a variety of staff serve on committees, providing a safeguard for maintaining fairness and objectivity in the classification of political activity and sensitive referrals.

RECOMMENDATIONS

To better ensure the Exempt Organization (EO) unit's adherence to the Tax Exempt and Government Entities (TE/GE) division's mission of "applying the tax law with integrity and fairness to all" in selecting exempt organizations to review or examine, we recommend that the Commissioner of Internal Revenue direct EO to take the following nine actions:

1) Complete the development and formally issue the Internal Revenue (IRM) sections on compliance checks and compliance reviews, and develop and formally issue an IRM section on Exempt Organization Compliance Area (EOCA) classification.
2) Develop, document, and implement a process to ensure that Internal Revenue Manual (IRM) sections and other procedures are reviewed and updated annually, and that updates reflect current practice, as required.
3) Develop, document, and implement additional monitoring procedures in order to ensure case selection controls, including ensuring that procedures for obtaining required signatures and documenting explanations for selection decisions, are being followed.
4) Develop, document, and implement procedures to ensure that all criteria or methods used in projects to select returns for examination are consistently documented and approved, including procedures related to documenting changes that occur during the course of a project, or new phases of a project.
5) Develop, document, and implement procedures for examination selection done by triage teams, including a process to consistently document selection criteria and triage team examination selection decisions.
6) Determine what additional controls may be needed to ensure examinations related to projects are properly coded.
7) For the databases EO uses during examination selection, develop complete and up to date data dictionaries to define data elements used in the databases.
8) Provide cross-training for referrals classifiers, prioritizing training for classifiers who work with political activity, high profile, and church referrals; and develop, document, and implement a system to ensure that those referrals are not always reviewed by the same classifier.

Selection process and primary source for procedures	Selection decision	Procedure	Effectiveness of procedure[a]	Error rate, cases failing to adhere to procedure	Sample or population size[b]	Confidenceinterval, forsamples
		Cases should have lead sheets (records used to gather research information and record the final conclusion for the case)	Effective	1 case	Population 3,230	N/A
		Cases should have final conclusions noted on their lead sheets	Indeterminate	3%	Sample 100	1–9%
		Lead sheets should align with disposal codes (codes used to note the decision on the case)	Indeterminate	5%	Sample 100	2–11%

Table 10. (Continued)

Selection process and primary source for procedures	**Selection decision**	**Procedure**	**Effectiveness of procedurea**	**Error rate, cases failing to adhere to procedure**	**Sample or population sizeb**	**Confidenceinterval, forsamples**
		On the Case Chronology Record, the findings should be explained and the final disposition of the review should be documented	Indeterminate but may be potential concern	6%	Sample 100	2–13%
		Lead sheets should be fully completed	Indeterminate but may be potential concern	6%	Sample 99	2–13%
EOCA Classification *EOCA classification procedures*	All	The classification input form should have a conclusion/summary of the classification process and, if an exam was recommended,	Indeterminate but may be potential concern	6%	Sample 86	2–13%

Selection process and primary source for procedures	Selection decision	Procedure	Effectiveness of procedure[a]	Error rate, cases failing to adhere to procedure	Sample or population size[b]	Confidenceinterval, forsamples
		should include a clear description of the issue				
		All of the questions on the main tab of the classification input form should be answered	Ineffective	13%	Sample 79	6–22%
Referrals *Referrals Procedures*	All	Referrals should have Case Chronology Records	Effective	0%	Population 5,317	N/A
	Selected	Actions on the referral reflect the classifier's determination	Effective	0%	Sample 89	0–3%

Table 10. (Continued)

Selection process and primary source for procedures	Selection decision	Procedure	Effectiveness of procedurea	Error rate, cases failing to adhere to procedure	Sample or population sizeb	Confidenceinterval, forsamples
		The classifier's determination for the referral should be consistent with the classifier's explanation[c]	Indeterminate	1%	Sample 84	0–7%
		Referrals selected for examination should be assigned a priority level	Effective	3%	Population 1,143	N/A
		Referrals should have an explanation for the classifier's determination in the comments field of the Referral Database	Indeterminate	3%	Sample 87	1–10%

Selection process and primary source for procedures	Selection decision	Procedure	Effectiveness of procedure[a]	Error rate, cases failing to adhere to procedure	Sample or population size[b]	Confidenceinterval, forsamples
		Classifiers sending referrals to the political activities, church, and high profile committees should provide a description of the allegation for the committee	Indeterminate but may be potential concern	4 out of 15 cases	N/A (sub-category)[d]	N/A
		Political activity referrals selected for examination contain a justification of the priority level that the Political Activities Referral Committee assigned the referral[c]	Indeterminate but may be potential concern	14 out of 14 cases	N/A (sub-category)[d]	N/A

Table 10. (Continued)

Selection process and primary source for procedures	**Selection decision**	**Procedure**	**Effectiveness of procedure**[a]	**Error rate, cases failing to adhere to procedure**	**Sample or population size**[b]	**Confidenceinterval, forsamples**
	Not selected	Actions on the referral reflect the classifier's determination	Effective	0%	Sample 94	0–3%
		Referrals should have an explanation for the classifier's determination in the comments field of the Referral Database[f]	Indeterminate but may be potential concern	9%	Sample 90	4-17%
		The classifier's determination for the referral should be consistent with the classifier's explanation[c]	Indeterminate	1%	Sample 91	0–6%

Selection process and primary source for procedures	**Selection decision**	**Procedure**	**Effectiveness of procedure**[a]	**Error rate, cases failing to adhere to procedure**	**Sample or population size**[b]	**Confidenceinterval, forsamples**
		Classifiers sending referrals to the political activities, church, and high profile committees should provide a description of the allegation for the committee	Indeterminate	0 out of 18 cases	N/A (sub-category)[d]	N/A
Examinations *Internal Revenue Manual*	Dismissed	Examinations that were dismissed must have explanations for the dismissal[g]	Ineffective	12%	Sample 66	5-23%
		Examinations that were dismissed must have management signatures[h]	Ineffective	22%	Sample 65	12-34%

Table 10. (Continued)

Selection process and primary source for procedures	Selection decision	Procedure	Effectiveness of procedure[a]	Error rate, cases failing to adhere to procedure	Sample or population size[b]	Confidenceinterval, forsamples
	Examined (Whistleblower)	Examinations that originated with whistleblower referrals must not contain forms or information that may identify a whistleblower[i]	Indeterminate but may be potential concern	3 out of 11 cases[j]	N/A[k]	N/A
	Examined (Claims)	Examinations that originated as claims should have a statement from the classifier about why the claim was sent for examination[l]	Ineffective	95%	Sample 76 claims	87-99%

Source: GAO analysis of IRS data. | GAO-15-514

Notes: We made our assessments based on requirements in effect in fiscal year 2014. We excluded certain file review findings because IRS told us that the requirements were obsolete, or because full information was not available to make the assessment.

[a]We used a tolerable error rate of 5 percent. For population-level tests, if the percentage of deviations from the procedure was less than or equal to 5 percent, we considered the procedure to have been implemented effectively. For random probability samples, if the upper bound of the 95 percent confidence interval for the estimated percentage of deviations from a procedure was less than or equal to 5 percent, we considered the procedure to have been implemented effectively, and if the lower bound of the confidence interval was greater than 5 percent, we considered the procedure to have been implemented ineffectively. If neither of these was the case, we considered our test to be statistically indeterminate.

[b]Sample and population sizes include cases where the procedure was implemented or not implemented; they exclude cases where the procedure was not applicable, or where we were unable to make a determination.

[c]This is not an explicit requirement in the *Referrals Procedures* document. However, the procedures do require the classifier to explain their determination for the referral. Therefore, we determined that it was reasonable to infer that the classifier's explanation should match his or her determination (decision) on the referral. If the two did not match, it may suggest an error in explaining the reason or coding the determination.

[d]We did not design our sample to support estimation for these sub-categories, so we are reporting out counts for what we found.

[e]Referrals procedures do not require a justification for the priority level. However, given that the priority level, as used in fiscal year 2014, could determine whether or not a referral is examined, a justification could be considered a significant event. Internal control standards require that significant events be clearly documented.

[f]We reviewed the classifier's comments to look for justification for the classification decision. Although 99 percent of referrals not selected for examination had some kind of text entered in the database box for classifier's comments, the text was not always descriptive. We did not count statements that simply said "no issue" as an explanation, as it does not describe what made the referral a "no issue" referral. This is in contrast to most of the referrals which included a description of the complaint or allegation against the organization and a reason why EO could not pursue the referral. For example, in one explanation, the classifier stated that the organization was not an exempt organization and was filing corporate returns, and in another referral, the classifier stated that the allegation was a management issue and there was nothing to substantiate that a tax law was violated.

[g]IRM Part 4, Chapter 75, Section 16. For claims, a dismissal means that adequate information was in the claim file to allow processing of the refund, credit, or adjustment.

[h]IRM Part 4, Chapter 75, Section 16.3.2.4.

[i]It is the examination team's responsibility to protect the identity and existence of the whistleblower from both the taxpayer and others without a need to know by segregating information about the whistleblower from the regular examination workpapers. This requirement is covered in IRM Part 4, Chapter 75, Section 4.7.5 and the 2014 Memorandum for Commissioner, Large Business and International; Commissioner, Small Business/Self-Employed; Commissioner, Tax Exempt and Government Entities; Chief, Criminal Investigation; Director, Whistleblower Office from Deputy Commissioner for Services and Enforcement, Internal Revenue Service, *IRS Whistleblower Program* (Aug. 20, 2014), at 2.

[j]In fiscal year 2014, EO closed 133 examinations that originated with whistleblowers. Three out of eleven cases we reviewed included information that could allow the whistleblower to be identified, such as the Social Security number and address for the whistleblower.

[k]The number of examination files that originated with whistleblower referrals that we reviewed was not designed to support estimation.

[l]IRM Part 4, Chapter 75, Section 4.5.2, Para. 2.A.

APPENDIX III: COMMENTS FROM THE INTERNAL REVENUE SERVICE

DEPARTMENT OF THE TREASURY
INTERNAL REVENUE SERVICE
WASHINGTON, D.C. 20224

DEPUTY COMMISSIONER

June 29, 2015

James R. McTigue, Jr.
Director, Tax Issues
United States Government Accountability Office
441 G Street, NW
Washington, DC 20548

Dear Mr. McTigue:

Thank you for the opportunity to review the draft report of the Government Accountability Office entitled "IRS Examination Selection: Internal Controls for Exempt Organization Selection Should Be Strengthened" (GAO-15-514, JC 451095). The draft report acknowledges that the IRS Exempt Organizations (EO) unit's reliance on a variety of sources to select returns for examination underscores our "recognition of the importance of having a robust and effective internal control system to ensure selection fairness and integrity." The draft report also makes recommendations for improvements to our database documentation, our referrals process, and IRS file tracking and maintenance. We have reviewed the draft report and, to the extent discussed in this letter, generally agree with its findings and recommendations. We have provided technical corrections and comments under separate cover.

EO continually strives to meet the Tax Exempt/Government Entities (TE/GE) Division's mission of applying the tax law with integrity and fairness to all. This is evident from the results of your focus groups with EO employees who conduct examinations and other reviews wherein you have observed that the employees "consistently equated fairness with assessing organizations strictly by whether they comply with tax law and with treating similar types of taxpayers equally."

We agree that internal controls are necessary to ensure that we meet our mission of applying the tax law with integrity and fairness. Although the report states that a hypothetical risk exists that returns could be selected unfairly, the draft report did not find any evidence that this has happened. Nevertheless, EO is committed to further strengthen our internal controls to ensure that we continue to select organizations for examination in a fair and consistent manner.

It is important to note that EO has taken measures consistent with your recommendations to update the EO Internal Revenue Manual (IRM) sections so that our employees have the guidance they need to carry out their responsibilities. We appreciate your acknowledgment that we maintain well-documented procedures for several examination selection processes, and that our employees use those procedures to conduct their work and view those procedures as valuable tools in carrying out their responsibilities.

In particular, the draft report states that guidance for the EO Compliance Area (EOCA) is not included in the IRM, but acknowledges that EO has developed applicable procedure documents outside of the IRM. The difference, according to the draft report, is that the IRM generally prohibits deviation from standard procedures, whereas a prohibition on deviation does not explicitly apply to the non-IRM procedure documents. As a practical matter, however, EO requires adherence to both the IRM and the non-IRM procedure documents, and the draft report does not identify any evidence of deviation from either source of guidance.

EO is in the second year of a three-year plan to update all 145 IRM sections that are applicable to EO. The draft report observes that some IRM provisions may become obsolete over time. As an example, the draft report acknowledges that an IRM provision that required stamping certain paper returns may have less relevance given the increasing incidence of electronic returns. Consequently, we continually update the IRM. New IRM sections are created as new processes are put into place. As examples, EO is currently developing IRM sections for the simplified and streamlined exemption application processes, the recently implemented post-determination process, and the new data-driven compliance strategy.

EO will continue to review and improve its efforts to maintain appropriate oversight of, and promote compliance by, the tax-exempt sector, including, in particular, our examination case selection internal control system. According to the draft report, many case referrals were not reviewed by the relevant committee assigned to review those referrals because the referrals raised "no issue." By design, classifiers review referrals – which could be complaints from members of the public not versed in tax law – to identify those that identify potential violations of the federal tax laws. If a referral poses a potential tax violation, it is referred to the appropriate committee. Committee review of referrals that do not identify federal tax issues would be inefficient and out of scope. Additionally, with respect to committee membership, the draft report notes that the referral committees are staffed by qualified employees who volunteer for this assignment with the expectation of being relieved of the assignment in 12 months. As committee workload has increased, fewer qualified employees have volunteered for this assignment and, as a result, this has extended the service of committee members. In recognition of this dynamic, EO plans to staff the referral committees by collateral assignment and not through the volunteer process on a going forward basis.

We appreciate having the opportunity to review and comment on the draft report. Responses to your specific recommendations are enclosed. If you have any questions, please contact me, or a member of your staff may contact Tamera Ripperda, Director, Exempt Organizations at (202) 317-8989.

Sincerely,

John M Dalrymple

John M. Dalrymple
Deputy Commissioner for Services and Enforcement

Enclosure

Enclosure

GAO Recommendations and IRS Responses to GAO Draft Report
IRS Examination Selection: Stronger Internal Controls Would Reduce Risk of Unfair Exempt Organization Selection

To better ensure EO adherence to TE/GE's mission of "applying the tax law with integrity and fairness to all" in selecting exempt organizations to review or examine, we recommend that the Commissioner of Internal Revenue direct EO to take the following 10 actions:

Recommendation 1: Complete the development and issue the IRM sections on compliance checks and compliance reviews, and develop and formally issue an IRM section on EOCA classification.

Comment: The Exempt Organizations Compliance Area (EOCA) has completed a draft IRM section that provides guidance on compliance checks and compliance reviews. This IRM section is currently under review and is expected to be finalized by October 2015. An IRM section on EOCA classification will be added to the IRM in Fiscal Year 2016.

Recommendation 2: Develop, document and implement a process to ensure that IRM sections and other procedures are reviewed and updated annually, and that updates reflect current practice, as required.

Comment: EO is currently in the second year of a three-year plan to update 100% of its IRM sections. EO Examinations is expected to complete its review and update 46 of the 62 IRM examination sections in FY 2015. The remaining sections are scheduled to be reviewed and updated in FY 2016. After all IRM examination sections have been updated, EO Examinations will review and update all the IRM examination sections on an annual basis.

Recommendation 3: Develop, document and implement additional monitoring procedures in order to ensure case selection controls, including ensuring that procedures for obtaining required signatures and documenting explanations for selection decisions, are being followed.

Comment: EO will review its current monitoring procedures, e.g., periodic sampling for required signatures and templates for approvals and explanations, and identify and implement any additional monitoring procedures that are needed to ensure case selection controls continue to be followed. The monitoring procedures will be reviewed through operational reviews by the appropriate EO executives. These reviews will document whether the appropriate documentation for case selection decisions is maintained and if periodic adjustments are needed.

Recommendation 4: Develop, document and implement procedures to ensure that all criteria or methods used in projects to select returns for examination are consistently documented and approved, including procedures related to documenting changes that occur during the course of a project, or new phases of a project.

Comment: Although EO is decreasing its focus on compliance projects, EO Examinations has begun following the Compliance Initiative Projects (CIP) IRM 4.17 to ensure that all criteria used to select returns for examination and executive approvals for added or changed criteria will be documented, including changes that occur during the project or in a new phase of a project.

Recommendation 5: Develop, document and implement procedures for examination selection done by triage teams, including a process to consistently document selection criteria and triage team examination selection decisions.

Comment: IRM sections are being written for the Compliance Strategies and Critical Initiatives (CSCI) and EOCA procedures for examination selection followed by triage teams, including a process to ensure the criteria and selection decisions are consistently documented.

Recommendation 6: Determine what additional controls may be needed to ensure examinations related to projects are properly coded.

Comment: In addition to continuing to monitor discrepancies and providing monthly reports to the Area Managers, EO will include a procedure in the CSCI IRM for these discrepancy reports and consider other controls that may be effective in addressing this issue.

Recommendation 7: For databases, EO uses during examination selection, develop data dictionaries to define data elements used in the databases.

Comment: For the two formal systems, Reporting Compliance Case Management System (RCCMS) and Return Inventory Classification System (RICS), EO will work with TE/GE Business Systems Planning (BSP) to propose a system change request to Information Technology (IT) in either creating (RCCMS) or updating (RICS) the associated system's dictionary. Finalizing these changes is subject to Information Technology resources. For the internal databases (EOCA and EOCA classification), as resources permit, EO will develop data dictionaries for these internal systems that will aid in the transitioning of the databases into RCCMS during FY 2016.

Recommendation 8: Provide cross-training for referrals classifiers, prioritizing training for classifiers who work with political activity, high profile, and church referrals; develop, document and implement a system to ensure that those referrals are not always reviewed by the same classifier.

Comment: EO will provide its classifiers with cross-training, prioritize the training of classifiers working with political activity, high profile and church referrals, and develop, document and implement a process to ensure that the referrals are reviewed on a rotating basis.

Recommendation 9: Ensure that referral committee members rotate every 12 months by soliciting volunteers. If EO does not believe that 12 months is an appropriate rotation length, then the IRM should be revised to require an alternative rotation schedule.

Comment: We will determine the appropriate rotation timeframe for the referral committee members, and will update our internal management documents, as necessary, for any changes.

Recommendation 10: Determine what additional controls may be needed to ensure that all closed examination files are tracked and maintained accurately.

Comment: EO will review, and if needed, clarify our internal processes within TE/GE regarding monitoring and shipping case files, and if necessary, will initiate discussions with Wage and Investment Files Office to clarify and improve the coordination between our business operating divisions with regard to the process of requesting, shipping, tracking and monitoring closed case files.

End Notes

[1] Gross domestic product is the market value of all goods and services produced within a country during a given time period. See McKeever, Brice S and Pettijohn, Sarah L., *The Nonprofit Sector in Brief 2014* (Washington D.C.: Urban Institute, October 2014); and Sherlock, Molly F. and Gravelle, Jane G., *An Overview of the Nonprofit and Charitable Sector*, CRS-R40919 (Washington, D.C.: Congressional Research Service, Nov. 17, 2009).

[2] Unrelated business income is the income from a trade or business regularly conducted by an exempt organization and not substantially related to the performance by the organization of its exempt purpose or function, except that the organization uses the profits derived from this activity. Certain trade or business activities are not treated as an unrelated trade or business. Organizations with $1,000 or more of gross income from unrelated businesses must report it on Form 990-T, *Exempt Organization Business Income Tax Return*.

[3] In the past, an inspector general report found that EO used inappropriate criteria to identify exempt organization applications for review. Our report does not cover EO's process for organizations applying for tax exempt status, it only covers examination selection of existing exempt organizations. Treasury Inspector General for Tax Administration, *Inappropriate Criteria Were Used to Identify Tax-Exempt Applications for Review*, 2013-10-053 (Washington, D.C: May 14, 2013).

[4] Internal Revenue Manual (IRM) Part 1, Chapter 1, Section 23.1 (the IRM can be accessed at http://www.irs.gov/irm/). TE/GE's mission, as set forth in the IRM, is "to provide its customers top quality service by helping them understand and comply with applicable tax laws and to protect the public interest by applying the tax law with integrity and fairness to all." TE/GE's mission closely aligns with the IRS-wide mission, as set forth in the IRS Strategic Plan for fiscal years 2014 to 2017, of providing "America's taxpayers top-quality service by helping them understand and meet their tax responsibilities and enforce the law with integrity and fairness to all." This report is the first of various reports on IRS examination and collection selection processes that we plan to issue this year.

[5] Classification is the process of identifying potential noncompliance in a return and making a recommendation on the examination potential for the return.

[6] IRM Part 1, Chapter 1, Section 23.1.

[7] GAO, *Standards for Internal Control in the Federal Government*, GAO-AIMD-00-21.3.1 (Washington, D.C.: November 1999).

[8] EO initiates projects that focus on specific areas of potential noncompliance (such as fundraising) or specific types of organizations (such as community foundations).

[9] Unless otherwise noted, all section numbers refer to the Internal Revenue Code found at Chapter 26 of the United States Code. Entities colloquially known as 501(c)(3) organizations are defined in the IRC as "corporations, and any community chest, fund, or foundations, organized and operated exclusively for religious, charitable, scientific, testing for public safety, literary, or educational purposes, or to foster national or international amateur sports competition, or for the prevention of cruelty to children or animals." 26 U.S.C.§ 501(c)(3). For more information on 501(c)(3) charitable organizations, see GAO, *Tax Exempt Organizations: Better Compliance Indicators and Data, and More Collaboration with State Regulators Would Strengthen Oversight of Charitable Organization*, GAO-15-164 (Washington, D.C.: Dec. 17, 2014).

[10] 26 U.S.C. §§ 521 and 527.

[11] 26 U.S.C. §§ 529-530.

[12] Exceptions to this requirement include churches and organizations (other than private charities) with annual gross receipts that are normally $5,000 or less. 26 U.S.C. 6033(a)(3). Also, section 501(c)(4), 501(c)(5), and 501(c)(6) organizations may "self declare" themselves to be exempt without filing an application. Although not a requirement, many of these organizations seek IRS exemption as an assurance for potential donors. Depending on the IRC section under which an exempt organization is seeking exemption, the organization will generally submit either Form 1023, *Application for Recognition of Exemption Under Section 501(c)(3) of the Internal Revenue Code*; Form 1023-EZ, *Streamlined Application for Recognition of Exemption Under Section 501(c)(3) of the Internal Revenue Code*; or Form 1024, *Application for Recognition of Exemption Under Section 501(a)*.

[13] Form 990, *Return of Organization Exempt from Income Tax,* Form 990-EZ, *Short Form Return of Organization Exempt from Income Tax,* or Form 990-PF, *Return of Private Foundation or Section 4947(a)(1) Trust Treated as Private Foundation*. Churches are not required to submit a Form 990. The term "churches" includes all similar religious houses of worship entities, such as mosques, temples, and synagogues, among other entities. Church is defined as including any organization claiming to be a church, and any convention or association of churches. 26 U.S.C. § 7611(h)(1).

[14] IRS does not have a particular term for such work. "Program" is our terminology.

[15] The Combined Annual Wage Reporting program is a document matching program that compares federal income tax withheld, Medicare wages, Social Security wages, and Social Security tips reported to IRS on employment tax returns against the amounts reported to the Social Security Administration via the processed totals of Form W-2 and other information returns. When this reconciliation results in an apparent underpayment of employment taxes or overwithholding of income tax, a Combined Annual Wage Reporting case is created.

[16] EO refers to these focus areas as "pillars."

[17] EO uses some proprietary third party databases of information which include public records.

[18] Compliance reviews are also used to gather information on certain organizations referred to EO as potentially noncompliant by the general public or another source. See below for further discussion on referrals.

[19] Cases that had compliance checks are classified by EOCA, and cases that had compliance reviews are classified by Exempt Organizations Examinations. If a case classified by EOCA meets certain criteria, it may be forwarded to Exempt Organization Examinations classification. Cases that had neither compliance reviews nor compliance checks may be classified by either group, depending on the details of the case. Returns classified by EOCA as having examination potential are generally sent for correspondence examinations conducted by EOCA. Returns classified by Exempt Organization Examinations as having examination potential are sent to Case Selection and Delivery and are generally conducted as field examinations.

[20] In fiscal year 2014, decisions were based on a priority list in a memorandum from the Director of EO Examinations. Memorandum for All EO Examinations Managers from Director, EO Examinations, Internal Revenue Service, *FY 2014 EO Examinations Program Priorities* (Oct. 17, 2013), at 2.

[21] Team Examination Program examinations typically involve significant resources and multiple team members, and may involve coordination with other IRS divisions. There were 269 Team Examination Program examinations initiated in fiscal year 2014. The IRM includes two criteria for including a return in the Team Examination Program: 1) for Form 990 filers, total income or beginning or end of year assets greater than $250 million, and 2) for Form

[72] According to EO officials, this project—which examines a sample of organizations that received a determination letter 5 years prior—was implemented in fiscal year 2005.

[73] For one of these projects, EO officials said that the box on the project proposal indicating a judgmental sample was to be used was erroneously checked, and that only a statistical sample was to be used.

[4] Projects using compliance checks and case building had already been using this document since around fiscal year 2010, according to EO officials.

[5] Triage teams are composed of subject matter experts, including project leads, analysts, and managers. They review the results of compliance checks or compliance reviews and, using their professional knowledge and expertise, apply project-specific criteria to make selection decisions.

Examination closures for projects are tracked using project codes, which correspond with codes used in the EO's annual examination work plan. A miscoding can occur if examination staff close a case and attribute it to the wrong project code.

IRM Part 2, Chapter 5, Section 13.1.

According to EO officials, in late March 2015 referrals classifiers began working new cases in RCCMS.

EO calls some of these systems inventory management databases; however, we consider them to be examination selection databases for the purposes of this report, as EO uses them to document examination selection decisions. According to EO officials, the RICS data dictionary was updated in 2005 and had a minor update in 2010, but is currently outdated.

Besides some data elements being defined in the EOCA procedures and job aid documents, several others are based on naming conventions outlined in an agency-wide reference document. Yet other data elements, such as those used for a quality review process, are defined in training documents.

ub. L. No. 107-347, 116 Stat. 2899, 44 U.S.C. 3501 note. Privacy Impact Assessments are intended to define how a system affects taxpayer or IRS employee privacy and can help eliminate unanticipated weaknesses in a system when conducted during the planning and design phases.

he Department of the Treasury and its various bureaus and offices, including IRS, refer to Privacy Impact Assessments as Privacy and Civil Liberties Impact Assessments. We use the term Privacy Impact Assessment as cited in the E-Government Act of 2002.

2013, the Treasury Inspector General of Tax Administration reported that IRS identified 184 systems and collections of information that required but did not have a Privacy Impact Assessment IRS agreed to review and take action on this deficiency. See Treasury Inspector General for Tax Administration, *Improvements are Needed to Ensure the Effectiveness of the Privacy Impact Assessment Process*, 2013-20-023 (Washington, D.C.: Feb. 27, 2013). A Treasury Inspector General of Tax Administration official reviewed the list of 184 databases for us and did not find these 3 EO databases on the list.

) receives referrals from IRS's Small Business/Self Employed Division, which processes forms from entities requesting determination of worker status for purposes of ascertaining the applicability of federal employment taxes and income tax withholding.

; described above, the five classifiers take turns sorting incoming referrals into categories based on an initial read of the referral.

ere may be several reasons why these referrals were not reviewed by a committee; however, a single classifier was the only person to review them.

990-PF and filers of Form 5227(*Split-Interest Trust Information Return*), income or end-of-year assets greater than $500 million (IRM Part 4, Chapter 75, Section 29.2). In addition to these criteria, project teams—such as triage teams—may identify returns to examine, in consultation with Team Examination Program staff. Team Examination Program examinations also occur when EO staff work with IRS's Large Business and International Division on an examination involving an exempt organization.

[22] IRS uses the term "survey" for examinations that are not initiated or not pursued after pre-examination reviews reveal a reason not to conduct the examination; the term is used IRS-wide. See IRM Part 4, Chapter 75, Section 16.3.2.

[23] The Internal Revenue Code has limitations on assessment and collection which require that the IRS assess, refund, credit, and collect taxes within specific time limits. See e.g., 26 U.S.C. §§ 6501, 7611(c)(1). Such a limit is called the statute of limitations. When it expires, IRS can no longer assess additional tax, allow a claim for refund by the taxpayer, or take collection action.

[24] Whistleblowers are individuals who spot problems in their workplace, while conducting day-to-day personal business, or anywhere else.

[25] The Tax Equity and Fiscal Responsibility Act of 1982, Pub. L. 97-248, 96 Stat. 324, (Sept. 3, 1982) established a complex set of examination, processing, and judicial procedures that affect the way IRS works with the partnerships and limited liability companies that file as partnerships and not with the separate partner level examinations. These referrals are reviewed to determine if any tax exempt partners need to be examined to reflect any adjustment made by the partnership.

[26] EO does not have a complete definition of "sensitive" referrals, although IRM Part 4, Chapter 75, Section 5 provides the example of the information submitted by an elected official (other than Congress or Executive Branch).

[27] IRM Part 4, Chapter 75, Section 5.6.

[28] If workload is heavy, the committee that reviews political activities identified through Form 990 queries will review political activity referrals, according to an EO official.

[29] The term Churches includes all similar religious houses of worship entities, such as mosques, temples, and synagogues, among other entities. Church is defined as including any organization claiming to be a church, and any convention or association of churches. 26 U.S.C. 7611(h)(1).

[30] The Referral Database does not have an identifier to differentiate between Church and High Profile Committee Referrals.

[31] IRS, Tax Exempt and Government Entities Division, *Exempt Organizations Referral Procedures* (revised September 2014).

[32] These criteria are the amount of money expended, size of audience for the alleged activity, significance of the political campaign, frequency of the alleged activity, degree of specificity to identify a candidate or the support/opposition, degree of candidate participation in the activity, and the degree to which the organization is soliciting contributions to support its political campaign activity.

[33] Memorandum for All EO Examinations Managers from Director, EO Examinations, Internal Revenue Service, *FY 2014 EO Examinations Program Priorities* (Oct. 17, 2013), at 2.

[34] 26 U.S.C. § 7611.

[35] 26 U.S.C. § 7611(a)(1)-(3).

[36] An excess benefit transaction is one in which an economic benefit is provided by an applicable tax-exempt organization, directly or indirectly, to or for the use of a disqualified person, and

the value of the economic benefit provided by the organization exceeds the value of the consideration received by the organization. A disqualified person is someone in a position to exercise substantial influence over the affairs of the applicable tax-exempt organization.

[37] An "appropriate high-level Treasury official" is defined as "the Secretary of the Treasury or any delegate of the Secretary whose rank is no lower than that of a principal Internal Revenue officer for an internal revenue region." 26 U.S.C. § 7611(h)(7).

[38] 26 U.S.C. § 7611(a)(2).

[39] IRM Part 4, Chapter 76, Section 7.5.2.

[40] IRM Part 4, Chapter 76, Section 7.5.

[41] 26 C.F.R. § 301.7611-1.

[42] We identified at least 72 referrals on potential political activity in churches in the Referral Database that were selected for examination by classifiers in fiscal year 2014 and 40 in fiscal 2013. Although selected by classifiers, these referrals would not necessarily become examinations, as they would need to follow the notice of inquiry procedures under IRC §7611. Also, between June 2013 and April 2014, EO suspended examinations on new political activity issues, while procedures related to political activity examinations were being reviewed and updated, according to EO officials. That hiatus likely also affected the number of church exams.

[43] Examinations on church noncompliance related to political activity issues, such as campaigning for a candidate, did not resume until April 2014, according to IRS officials, when EO resumed examinations that were previously started and suspended on political activity allegations.

[44] *United States v. Living Word Christian Center*, 103 AFTR 2d 714, Civil No. 08-mc-37 ADM/JJK, D.Minn. (Jan. 30, 2009).

[45] IRS established that an appropriate high-level Treasury official was a "Regional Commissioner (or higher Treasury official)." 26 C.F.R. § 301.7611-1, Q&A (1). However, the Internal Revenue Service Restructuring and Reform Act of 1998, Pub. L. No. 105-206, § 1001(a), 112 Stat. 685 (1998), eliminated the position of Regional Commissioner. IRS officials stated that starting in 2013, the review process changed and the Director of Exempt Organizations solicited the review and concurrence of the TE/GE Commissioner.

[46] *Amendments to the Regulations Regarding Questions and Answers Relating to Church Tax Inquiries and Examinations*, 74 Fed. Reg. 39,003 (Aug. 5, 2009).

[47] In April 2015, a Freedom of Information Act lawsuit was filed in the U.S. District Court for the District of Columbia, against the IRS by an entity called Alliance Defending Freedom, for the failure to release documents related to church inquiries and examinations since January 2009, and documents related to 26 C.F.R. § 301.7611-1. *Alliance Defending Freedom v. IRS* (No. 1:15-cv-00525).

[48] IRM Part 25, Chapter 1, Section 2 and IRM Part 4, Chapter 75, Section 21.8.

[49] The Criminal Investigation division is not part of TE/GE, but they do investigate cases involving exempt organizations.

[50] IRM Part 1, Chapter 11, Section 2.2

[51] We consider examinations to be case selection processes because examinations may be dismissed and examinations may be expanded to include related pickups and substitutes for returns.

[52] EO officials provided us complete drafts of two IRM sections in April 2015. One IRM section, the Small Business/Self-Employed division's IRM for Compliance Initiative Projects (IRM Part 4, Chapter 17, Sections 1.1 - 4.11), is being revised to incorporate EO language and

contains procedures for developing, approving, and managing Complia
Projects, which will include EO projects and queries. The second IRM sectic
Chapter 75 Section 8) is a new EO-specific section on projects and querie
specific roles and responsibilities of certain EO staff during this process.

[53] Our tests for Case Chronology Records for both EOCA and referrals were p
tests of cases closed fiscal year 2014. For EOCA, each of 5,242 cases had C
Records. For referrals, each of 5,317 cases had Case Chronology Records.

[54] IRM Part 1, Chapter 2, Section 13.1.5.

[55] IRM Part 1, Chapter 2, Section 13.1.5.

[56] IRM Part 1, Chapter 11, Section 2.2.

[57] 5 U.S.C. § 552(a)(2)(c).

[58] IRM Part 1, Chapter 11, Section 1.6.5.

[59] IRM Part 1, Chapter 11, Section 2.2.1.

[60] IRM Part 4, Chapter 75, Section 29.2. The IRM refers to the standardized crit
Examination Program as "bright line standards."

[61] IRM Part 4, Chapter 75, Sections 16.3.2.1 and 16.3.2.2.

[62] IRM Part 4, Chapter 75, Section 12.9.

[63] RCCMS is an information system that supports examination selection a
providing case management, inventory control and routing capabilities. N
notice within RCCMS, though an email-like prompt, that examination st
approval for a related-pickup.

[64] The 95 percent confidence interval for this estimate is (12 percent, 34 percen

[65] GAO, *Tax Administration: The Internal Revenue Service Can Improve*
Paper Case Files, GAO-07-1160 (Washington D.C., September 2007).
did not have an effective process to ensure that paper case files can b
requesters' time frames; however, this review did not include TE/GE
recommendations, which IRS implemented.

[66] IRM Part 1, Chapter 15, Section 1.4.

[67] EO officials said they completed forms showing that the completed case f
and received by the IRS unit in charge of storing them. Once the ack
the files are received, EO no longer has jurisdiction over them.

[68] The 95 percent confidence interval around this estimate is 7 percen
requested 100 closed examination files. EO provided 87 files but wa
files in a timely manner. Ten of 13 files not located in a timely manne
for examinations that originated as related pick-ups; the other 2 were
for refunds.

[69] Here we use the term projects broadly to include Form 990 analytic
deemed successful and continued on an ongoing basis, unless otherwi

[70] For example, the latter types of projects require that project teams devel

[71] We reviewed a purposive sample (a type of non-probability sample) of
closed in fiscal year 2014. These projects were selected to cover a v
of number of cases closed), ages (in terms of project start dates), ty
used a query or not), and other factors. We did not review the p
original 13 projects in our sample because EO officials told us that
active in fiscal year 2014, as further described below. These 11
2,100 examinations closed and about 2,700 other types of revie
2014.

9) Ensure that referral committee members rotate every 12 months by soliciting volunteers. If EO does not believe that 12 months is an appropriate rotation length, then the Internal Revenue Manual (IRM) should be revised to require an alternative rotation schedule.

In addition, we recommend that the Commissioner of Internal Revenue take the following action:

1. Determine what additional controls may be needed to ensure that all closed examination files are tracked and maintained accurately.

AGENCY COMMENTS AND OUR EVALUATION

We provided a draft of this report to IRS for review and comment. In its written comments, reproduced in appendix III, IRS generally agreed with our findings and recommendations. In its comments, IRS described the steps it plans to take to implement the recommendations. IRS also provided technical comments, which we incorporated where appropriate.

James R. McTigue, Jr.
Director,
Tax Issues Strategic Issues

APPENDIX I: OBJECTIVES, SCOPE, AND METHODOLOGY

This report (1) describes the processes for selecting tax-exempt organizations for examination, and (2) assesses the adequacy of the controls (including procedures) for selecting examination cases that the Exempt Organizations (EO) unit uses to achieve the Tax Exempt and Government Entities (TE/GE) division's stated mission of "applying the tax law with integrity and fairness to all."

For the first objective, we reviewed Internal Revenue Service (IRS) documents that describe the processes and criteria for selecting exempt organization returns for examination. These documents included sections of the Internal Revenue Manual (IRM), procedures documents, training documents, worksheets for reviewing files, and summaries of selection processes prepared by EO officials. We also interviewed IRS officials responsible for overseeing examination selection. In addition, we obtained data from the following IRS databases: Returns Inventory and Classification System (RICS), Referral database, Exempt Organizations Compliance Area (EOCA) database, and EOCA Classification database. The databases contain information on initiated and closed examinations, classification of referrals, and compliance reviews and compliance checks.[1] Based on our testing of the data and review of documentation and interviews, we determined that these data were reliable for the purposes of this report.

For the second objective, we reviewed EO's examination selection procedures and related internal controls intended to help TE/GE achieve its stated mission of "enforcing the tax law with integrity and fairness to all."[2] We then assessed whether these procedures followed standards from *Standards for Internal Control in the Federal Government* that were relevant to examination case selection.[3] We also conducted six focus groups with selected EO staff who are responsible for selecting, or doing research to help select, exempt organization returns for examination, and two focus groups of selected EO staff who conduct examinations.[4] In total, our groups involved 41 participants with an average of about 17 years of IRS experience, with a range from 8 months to 37 years of experience. The focus groups were held at IRS offices in Ogden, Utah; Dallas; and Atlanta. We asked questions on internal control related topics, such as the clarity of EO procedures and the adequacy of training to apply these procedures. We used NVivo qualitative data analysis software to conduct a content analysis of themes from the focus groups.

To assess how well EO implemented its procedures and applied examination selection criteria, we used IRM sections, EO procedures documents, and other documents as criteria. We reviewed the populations of cases or referrals closed during fiscal year 2014 in the Referral, EOCA, and EOCA Classification databases.[5] Within the populations, we looked for completeness of required fields used in conducting research or selecting returns for examination. For our population-level analyses, we considered any control with a nonadherence rate greater than 5 percent to be ineffective. We also selected random probability samples of the database files to review required text, such as justifications for selecting or not selecting a return for examination or review. Finally, we selected random probability samples of dismissed examination files, and closed examination files from processes described earlier in this report.[6] Table 9 summarizes the probability samples we reviewed.

Table 9. Exempt Organizations (EO) Selection Processes, Population, and Sample Descriptions

Selection process	Selection decision	Records we reviewed	Unit of analysis	Population size (closed in fiscal year 2014)	Sample size (closed in fiscal year 2014)
Exempt Organizations Compliance Area (EOCA) – Compliance checks and compliance reviews	All	EOCA database	Organization	5,242	100
EOCA Classification	All	EOCA classification database	Tax return	2,355	100
Referrals processing[a]	Selected for examination	Referral database	Referral	1,143	89
Referrals processing	Not selected for examination	Referral database	Referral	4,173	94
Examinations[b]	Dismissed	Paper and electronic case files	Tax return	1,858	100
	Examined	Paper and electronic case files	Tax return	606 c	100

Source: GAO analysis of IRS data. | GAO-15-514.

NOTES:

[a]We selected a stratified random sample in order to have generalizable samples for referrals based on whether they were selected for examination or not. We included referrals selected for compliance reviews, compliance checks, transfers, and future year referrals in the population of referrals not selected for examination.

[b]We consider examinations to be case selection processes because examinations may be dismissed, and related pick-ups and substitutes for return may be developed in the course of examinations.

[c]We excluded certain closed examination cases from our review population: we excluded examination cases originating from referrals and EOCA processes because we reviewed those processes directly, we excluded cases for which no staff discretion was involved, and we excluded cases of limited value to our sample for other reasons. Therefore, the examination population number presented here will not match up with elsewhere in our report.

The file and database review samples were obtained by following a probability procedure based on the selection of random samples. The database and examination files we reviewed were closed in fiscal year 2014, and we assessed them against requirements that were in effect during that time. For the populations and samples we reviewed, we used a 5 percent tolerable error rate to assess the adequacy of internal controls. Within the probability samples, we reviewed certain controls that were only applicable to a subgroup of the files in the sample. We reported on problems identified in those subgroups, but we did not design our samples to support estimation for those sub-categories. In those cases, we present our results as numbers of instances where the control was not effective.

Because we followed a probability procedure based on random selections, our sample is only one of a large number of samples that we might have drawn. Since each sample could have provided different estimates, we express our confidence in the precision of our particular sample's results as a 95 percent confidence interval (e.g., plus-or-minus 10 percentage points). This is the interval that would contain the actual population value for 95 percent of the samples we could have drawn. For our random probability samples, we considered a control to be ineffective if the entirety of the confidence interval around our estimated nonadherence rate was greater than 5 percent, and to be effective if the entirety of the confidence interval was less than or equal to 5 percent. If the confidence interval overlapped 5 percent, we considered our test to be inconclusive.

We also reviewed a non-generalizable sample of 11 projects that were active during fiscal year 2014.[7] We selected those projects to include a variety of sizes (based on number of returns examined), ages (start dates for the project), as well as some projects that relied on Form 990 data queries and politically sensitive projects. We reviewed the project files for each project to test whether the documentation—such as development and approval of examination selection criteria—followed project development procedures. We also reviewed a non-generalizable sample of 11 closed examination files that originated with whistleblowers to check that IRM and referrals procedures were followed with regard to ensuring whistleblower information is not kept in the examination file. Finally, we interviewed EO officials about the processes and discussed deficiencies we identified.

We designed uniform data collection instruments for our file and database reviews to consistently capture information on the completeness of required documentation and approvals related to case selection. IRS verified the criteria we used in our instruments, and identified any outdated criteria we had

[87] IRM Part 4, Chapter 75, Section 5.6.

[88] We compared the start dates provided by IRS with activity from each committee member documented in the Referrals Database. We found that, in general, the dates IRS provided align with activity recorded in the database.

[89] IRM Part 4, Chapter 75, Section 5.6.

[90] EO drafted a memorandum in February 2014, but it was never issued.

End Notes for Appendix I

[1] A compliance review determines whether an organization is operating in accordance with its exempt purpose and is current with its filing requirements, based on document review and research without direct taxpayer contact. A compliance check is a correspondence contact with an organization to inquire about compliance.

[2] IRM, Part 1, Chapter 1, Section 23.

[3] GAO, *Standards for Internal Control in the Federal Government*, GAO-AIMD-00-21.3 (Washington, D.C., November 1999).

[4] For the six groups of staff who work in the examination selection process, who were located in Ogden, Utah; Dallas; and Atlanta, we were able to invite all staff, with exception of one group where we randomly selected participants in order to have a manageable group size. Staff who conduct examinations are located all over the country. We invited all examination staff based in Dallas for the two relevant focus groups so that we could conduct the groups in person.

[5] The Referral Database contains records of all referrals received in EO, including those that were mistakenly sent to EO (misroutes) and those that do have not have enough information to classify (no issue referrals). For other referrals, the database serves as a log of actions on a referral, including the classification decision and explanation for the decision. In our population and samples, we only reviewed referrals that completed the classification process in fiscal year 2014. We excluded duplicate referrals (referrals on the same issue for an organization), misroutes, and referrals that were still being classified. The EOCA Database contains records of all compliance review and compliance check cases worked by EOCA. We only reviewed cases that were closed in fiscal year 2014. We excluded reviews of operations performed for the Patient Protection and Affordable Care Act because there were no selection decisions related to those reviews. The EOCA Classification Database contains records of all tax returns classified by EOCA. We only reviewed cases that were closed in fiscal year 2014.

[6] Once an examination is sent to an examination group, the manager or examination staff may dismiss the return from examination. Typically, this is done because a return is nearing the date that limits the time period during which IRS may impose taxes or penalties on the return, based on statutory requirements.

[7] EO initiates projects that focus on specific areas of potential noncompliance (such as fundraising) or specific types of organizations (such as community foundations).

End Note for Appendix II

[1]There were a few situations in which we could not make a conclusive determination about whether implementation was successful. We reviewed certain sub-categories of samples, and we did not design our samples to support estimation for these subcategories. Similarly, in the case of examination files that originated with whistleblower referrals, we reviewed a number of files that was not designed to support estimation. Additionally, in some cases, the 95 percent confidence intervals around our estimates overlapped the 5 percent tolerable error rate.

990-PF and filers of Form 5227(*Split-Interest Trust Information Return*), income or end-of-year assets greater than $500 million (IRM Part 4, Chapter 75, Section 29.2). In addition to these criteria, project teams—such as triage teams—may identify returns to examine, in consultation with Team Examination Program staff. Team Examination Program examinations also occur when EO staff work with IRS's Large Business and International Division on an examination involving an exempt organization.

[22] IRS uses the term "survey" for examinations that are not initiated or not pursued after pre-examination reviews reveal a reason not to conduct the examination; the term is used IRS-wide. See IRM Part 4, Chapter 75, Section 16.3.2.

[23] The Internal Revenue Code has limitations on assessment and collection which require that the IRS assess, refund, credit, and collect taxes within specific time limits. See e.g., 26 U.S.C. §§ 6501, 7611(c)(1). Such a limit is called the statute of limitations. When it expires, IRS can no longer assess additional tax, allow a claim for refund by the taxpayer, or take collection action.

[24] Whistleblowers are individuals who spot problems in their workplace, while conducting day-to-day personal business, or anywhere else.

[25] The Tax Equity and Fiscal Responsibility Act of 1982, Pub. L. 97-248, 96 Stat. 324, (Sept. 3, 1982) established a complex set of examination, processing, and judicial procedures that affect the way IRS works with the partnerships and limited liability companies that file as partnerships and not with the separate partner level examinations. These referrals are reviewed to determine if any tax exempt partners need to be examined to reflect any adjustment made by the partnership.

[26] EO does not have a complete definition of "sensitive" referrals, although IRM Part 4, Chapter 75, Section 5 provides the example of the information submitted by an elected official (other than Congress or Executive Branch).

[27] IRM Part 4, Chapter 75, Section 5.6.

[28] If workload is heavy, the committee that reviews political activities identified through Form 990 queries will review political activity referrals, according to an EO official.

[29] The term Churches includes all similar religious houses of worship entities, such as mosques, temples, and synagogues, among other entities. Church is defined as including any organization claiming to be a church, and any convention or association of churches. 26 U.S.C. 7611(h)(1).

[30] The Referral Database does not have an identifier to differentiate between Church and High Profile Committee Referrals.

[31] IRS, Tax Exempt and Government Entities Division, *Exempt Organizations Referral Procedures* (revised September 2014).

[32] These criteria are the amount of money expended, size of audience for the alleged activity, significance of the political campaign, frequency of the alleged activity, degree of specificity to identify a candidate or the support/opposition, degree of candidate participation in the activity, and the degree to which the organization is soliciting contributions to support its political campaign activity.

[33] Memorandum for All EO Examinations Managers from Director, EO Examinations, Internal Revenue Service, *FY 2014 EO Examinations Program Priorities* (Oct. 17, 2013), at 2.

[34] 26 U.S.C. § 7611.

[35] 26 U.S.C. § 7611(a)(1)-(3).

[36] An excess benefit transaction is one in which an economic benefit is provided by an applicable tax-exempt organization, directly or indirectly, to or for the use of a disqualified person, and

the value of the economic benefit provided by the organization exceeds the value of the consideration received by the organization. A disqualified person is someone in a position to exercise substantial influence over the affairs of the applicable tax-exempt organization.

[37] An "appropriate high-level Treasury official" is defined as "the Secretary of the Treasury or any delegate of the Secretary whose rank is no lower than that of a principal Internal Revenue officer for an internal revenue region." 26 U.S.C. § 7611(h)(7).

[38] 26 U.S.C. § 7611(a)(2).

[39] IRM Part 4, Chapter 76, Section 7.5.2.

[40] IRM Part 4, Chapter 76, Section 7.5.

[41] 26 C.F.R. § 301.7611-1.

[42] We identified at least 72 referrals on potential political activity in churches in the Referral Database that were selected for examination by classifiers in fiscal year 2014 and 40 in fiscal 2013. Although selected by classifiers, these referrals would not necessarily become examinations, as they would need to follow the notice of inquiry procedures under IRC §7611. Also, between June 2013 and April 2014, EO suspended examinations on new political activity issues, while procedures related to political activity examinations were being reviewed and updated, according to EO officials. That hiatus likely also affected the number of church exams.

[43] Examinations on church noncompliance related to political activity issues, such as campaigning for a candidate, did not resume until April 2014, according to IRS officials, when EO resumed examinations that were previously started and suspended on political activity allegations.

[44] *United States v. Living Word Christian Center*, 103 AFTR 2d 714, Civil No. 08-mc-37 ADM/JJK, D.Minn. (Jan. 30, 2009).

[45] IRS established that an appropriate high-level Treasury official was a "Regional Commissioner (or higher Treasury official)." 26 C.F.R. § 301.7611-1, Q&A (1). However, the Internal Revenue Service Restructuring and Reform Act of 1998, Pub. L. No. 105-206, § 1001(a), 112 Stat. 685 (1998), eliminated the position of Regional Commissioner. IRS officials stated that starting in 2013, the review process changed and the Director of Exempt Organizations solicited the review and concurrence of the TE/GE Commissioner.

[46] *Amendments to the Regulations Regarding Questions and Answers Relating to Church Tax Inquiries and Examinations*, 74 Fed. Reg. 39,003 (Aug. 5, 2009).

[47] In April 2015, a Freedom of Information Act lawsuit was filed in the U.S. District Court for the District of Columbia, against the IRS by an entity called Alliance Defending Freedom, for the failure to release documents related to church inquiries and examinations since January 2009, and documents related to 26 C.F.R. § 301.7611-1. *Alliance Defending Freedom v. IRS* (No. 1:15-cv-00525).

[48] IRM Part 25, Chapter 1, Section 2 and IRM Part 4, Chapter 75, Section 21.8.

[49] The Criminal Investigation division is not part of TE/GE, but they do investigate cases involving exempt organizations.

[50] IRM Part 1, Chapter 11, Section 2.2

[51] We consider examinations to be case selection processes because examinations may be dismissed and examinations may be expanded to include related pickups and substitutes for returns.

[52] EO officials provided us complete drafts of two IRM sections in April 2015. One IRM section, the Small Business/Self-Employed division's IRM for Compliance Initiative Projects (IRM Part 4, Chapter 17, Sections 1.1 - 4.11), is being revised to incorporate EO language and

contains procedures for developing, approving, and managing Compliance Initiative Projects, which will include EO projects and queries. The second IRM section (IRM Part 4 Chapter 75 Section 8) is a new EO-specific section on projects and queries that outlines specific roles and responsibilities of certain EO staff during this process.

[53] Our tests for Case Chronology Records for both EOCA and referrals were population-level tests of cases closed fiscal year 2014. For EOCA, each of 5,242 cases had Case Chronology Records. For referrals, each of 5,317 cases had Case Chronology Records.

[54] IRM Part 1, Chapter 2, Section 13.1.5.

[55] IRM Part 1, Chapter 2, Section 13.1.5.

[56] IRM Part 1, Chapter 11, Section 2.2.

[57] 5 U.S.C. § 552(a)(2)(c).

[58] IRM Part 1, Chapter 11, Section 1.6.5.

[59] IRM Part 1, Chapter 11, Section 2.2.1.

[60] IRM Part 4, Chapter 75, Section 29.2. The IRM refers to the standardized criteria for the Team Examination Program as "bright line standards."

[61] IRM Part 4, Chapter 75, Sections 16.3.2.1 and 16.3.2.2.

[62] IRM Part 4, Chapter 75, Section 12.9.

[63] RCCMS is an information system that supports examination selection and processing by providing case management, inventory control and routing capabilities. Managers receive a notice within RCCMS, though an email-like prompt, that examination staff have requested approval for a related-pickup.

[64] The 95 percent confidence interval for this estimate is (12 percent, 34 percent).

[65] GAO, *Tax Administration: The Internal Revenue Service Can Improve Its Management of Paper Case Files*, GAO-07-1160 (Washington D.C., September 2007). We found that IRS did not have an effective process to ensure that paper case files can be located within the requesters' time frames; however, this review did not include TE/GE files. We made five recommendations, which IRS implemented.

[66] IRM Part 1, Chapter 15, Section 1.4.

[67] EO officials said they completed forms showing that the completed case files were transferred and received by the IRS unit in charge of storing them. Once the acknowledged forms for the files are received, EO no longer has jurisdiction over them.

[68] The 95 percent confidence interval around this estimate is 7 percent to 21 percent. We requested 100 closed examination files. EO provided 87 files but was unable to locate 13 files in a timely manner. Ten of 13 files not located in a timely manner were electronic files for examinations that originated as related pick-ups; the other 2 were paper files for claims for refunds.

[69] Here we use the term projects broadly to include Form 990 analytics queries and projects deemed successful and continued on an ongoing basis, unless otherwise noted in the text.

[70] For example, the latter types of projects require that project teams develop training materials.

[71] We reviewed a purposive sample (a type of non-probability sample) of projects that had cases closed in fiscal year 2014. These projects were selected to cover a variety of sizes (in terms of number of cases closed), ages (in terms of project start dates), type of project (whether it used a query or not), and other factors. We did not review the project files for 2 of the original 13 projects in our sample because EO officials told us that these projects were not active in fiscal year 2014, as further described below. These 11 projects represent about 2,100 examinations closed and about 2,700 other types of reviews closed in fiscal year 2014.

[72] According to EO officials, this project—which examines a sample of organizations that received a determination letter 5 years prior—was implemented in fiscal year 2005.

[73] For one of these projects, EO officials said that the box on the project proposal indicating a judgmental sample was to be used was erroneously checked, and that only a statistical sample was to be used.

[74] Projects using compliance checks and case building had already been using this document since around fiscal year 2010, according to EO officials.

[75] Triage teams are composed of subject matter experts, including project leads, analysts, and managers. They review the results of compliance checks or compliance reviews and, using their professional knowledge and expertise, apply project-specific criteria to make selection decisions.

[76] Examination closures for projects are tracked using project codes, which correspond with codes used in the EO's annual examination work plan. A miscoding can occur if examination staff close a case and attribute it to the wrong project code.

[77] IRM Part 2, Chapter 5, Section 13.1.

[78] According to EO officials, in late March 2015 referrals classifiers began working new cases in RCCMS.

[79] EO calls some of these systems inventory management databases; however, we consider them to be examination selection databases for the purposes of this report, as EO uses them to document examination selection decisions. According to EO officials, the RICS data dictionary was updated in 2005 and had a minor update in 2010, but is currently outdated.

[80] Besides some data elements being defined in the EOCA procedures and job aid documents, several others are based on naming conventions outlined in an agency-wide reference document. Yet other data elements, such as those used for a quality review process, are defined in training documents.

[81] Pub. L. No. 107-347, 116 Stat. 2899, 44 U.S.C. 3501 note. Privacy Impact Assessments are intended to define how a system affects taxpayer or IRS employee privacy and can help eliminate unanticipated weaknesses in a system when conducted during the planning and design phases.

[82] The Department of the Treasury and its various bureaus and offices, including IRS, refer to Privacy Impact Assessments as Privacy and Civil Liberties Impact Assessments. We use the term Privacy Impact Assessment as cited in the E-Government Act of 2002.

[83] In 2013, the Treasury Inspector General of Tax Administration reported that IRS identified 184 systems and collections of information that required but did not have a Privacy Impact Assessment IRS agreed to review and take action on this deficiency. See Treasury Inspector General for Tax Administration, *Improvements are Needed to Ensure the Effectiveness of the Privacy Impact Assessment Process*, 2013-20-023 (Washington, D.C.: Feb. 27, 2013). A Treasury Inspector General of Tax Administration official reviewed the list of 184 databases for us and did not find these 3 EO databases on the list.

[84] EO receives referrals from IRS's Small Business/Self Employed Division, which processes forms from entities requesting determination of worker status for purposes of ascertaining the applicability of federal employment taxes and income tax withholding.

[85] As described above, the five classifiers take turns sorting incoming referrals into categories based on an initial read of the referral.

[86] There may be several reasons why these referrals were not reviewed by a committee; however, a single classifier was the only person to review them.

9) Ensure that referral committee members rotate every 12 months by soliciting volunteers. If EO does not believe that 12 months is an appropriate rotation length, then the Internal Revenue Manual (IRM) should be revised to require an alternative rotation schedule.

In addition, we recommend that the Commissioner of Internal Revenue take the following action:

1. Determine what additional controls may be needed to ensure that all closed examination files are tracked and maintained accurately.

Agency Comments and Our Evaluation

We provided a draft of this report to IRS for review and comment. In its written comments, reproduced in appendix III, IRS generally agreed with our findings and recommendations. In its comments, IRS described the steps it plans to take to implement the recommendations. IRS also provided technical comments, which we incorporated where appropriate.

James R. McTigue, Jr.
Director,
Tax Issues Strategic Issues

Appendix I: Objectives, Scope, and Methodology

This report (1) describes the processes for selecting tax-exempt organizations for examination, and (2) assesses the adequacy of the controls (including procedures) for selecting examination cases that the Exempt Organizations (EO) unit uses to achieve the Tax Exempt and Government Entities (TE/GE) division's stated mission of "applying the tax law with integrity and fairness to all."

For the first objective, we reviewed Internal Revenue Service (IRS) documents that describe the processes and criteria for selecting exempt organization returns for examination. These documents included sections of the Internal Revenue Manual (IRM), procedures documents, training documents, worksheets for reviewing files, and summaries of selection processes prepared by EO officials. We also interviewed IRS officials responsible for overseeing examination selection. In addition, we obtained data from the following IRS databases: Returns Inventory and Classification System (RICS), Referral database, Exempt Organizations Compliance Area (EOCA) database, and EOCA Classification database. The databases contain information on initiated and closed examinations, classification of referrals, and compliance reviews and compliance checks.[1] Based on our testing of the data and review of documentation and interviews, we determined that these data were reliable for the purposes of this report.

For the second objective, we reviewed EO's examination selection procedures and related internal controls intended to help TE/GE achieve its stated mission of "enforcing the tax law with integrity and fairness to all."[2] We then assessed whether these procedures followed standards from *Standards for Internal Control in the Federal Government* that were relevant to examination case selection.[3] We also conducted six focus groups with selected EO staff who are responsible for selecting, or doing research to help select, exempt organization returns for examination, and two focus groups of selected EO staff who conduct examinations.[4] In total, our groups involved 41 participants with an average of about 17 years of IRS experience, with a range from 8 months to 37 years of experience. The focus groups were held at IRS offices in Ogden, Utah; Dallas; and Atlanta. We asked questions on internal control related topics, such as the clarity of EO procedures and the adequacy of training to apply these procedures. We used NVivo qualitative data analysis software to conduct a content analysis of themes from the focus groups.

To assess how well EO implemented its procedures and applied examination selection criteria, we used IRM sections, EO procedures documents, and other documents as criteria. We reviewed the populations of cases or referrals closed during fiscal year 2014 in the Referral, EOCA, and EOCA Classification databases.[5] Within the populations, we looked for completeness of required fields used in conducting research or selecting returns for examination. For our population-level analyses, we considered any control with a nonadherence rate greater than 5 percent to be ineffective. We also selected random probability samples of the database files to review required text, such as justifications for selecting or not selecting a return for examination or review. Finally, we selected random probability samples of dismissed examination files, and closed examination files from processes described earlier in this report.[6] Table 9 summarizes the probability samples we reviewed.

Table 9. Exempt Organizations (EO) Selection Processes, Population, and Sample Descriptions

Selection process	Selection decision	Records we reviewed	Unit of analysis	Population size (closed in fiscal year 2014)	Sample size (closed in fiscal year 2014)
Exempt Organizations Compliance Area (EOCA) – Compliance checks and compliance reviews	All	EOCA database	Organizatio n	5,242	100
EOCA Classification	All	EOCA classification database	Tax return	2,355	100
Referrals processing[a]	Selected for examination	Referral database	Referral	1,143	89
Referrals processing	Not selected for examination	Referral database	Referral	4,173	94
Examinations[b]	Dismissed	Paper and electronic case files	Tax return	1,858	100
	Examined	Paper and electronic case files	Tax return	606 c	100

Source: GAO analysis of IRS data. | GAO-15-514.

NOTES:

[a]We selected a stratified random sample in order to have generalizable samples for referrals based on whether they were selected for examination or not. We included referrals selected for compliance reviews, compliance checks, transfers, and future year referrals in the population of referrals not selected for examination.

[b]We consider examinations to be case selection processes because examinations may be dismissed, and related pick-ups and substitutes for return may be developed in the course of examinations.

[c]We excluded certain closed examination cases from our review population: we excluded examination cases originating from referrals and EOCA processes because we reviewed those processes directly, we excluded cases for which no staff discretion was involved, and we excluded cases of limited value to our sample for other reasons. Therefore, the examination population number presented here will not match up with elsewhere in our report.

The file and database review samples were obtained by following a probability procedure based on the selection of random samples. The database and examination files we reviewed were closed in fiscal year 2014, and we assessed them against requirements that were in effect during that time. For the populations and samples we reviewed, we used a 5 percent tolerable error rate to assess the adequacy of internal controls. Within the probability samples, we reviewed certain controls that were only applicable to a subgroup of the files in the sample. We reported on problems identified in those subgroups, but we did not design our samples to support estimation for those sub-categories. In those cases, we present our results as numbers of instances where the control was not effective.

Because we followed a probability procedure based on random selections, our sample is only one of a large number of samples that we might have drawn. Since each sample could have provided different estimates, we express our confidence in the precision of our particular sample's results as a 95 percent confidence interval (e.g., plus-or-minus 10 percentage points). This is the interval that would contain the actual population value for 95 percent of the samples we could have drawn. For our random probability samples, we considered a control to be ineffective if the entirety of the confidence interval around our estimated nonadherence rate was greater than 5 percent, and to be effective if the entirety of the confidence interval was less than or equal to 5 percent. If the confidence interval overlapped 5 percent, we considered our test to be inconclusive.

We also reviewed a non-generalizable sample of 11 projects that were active during fiscal year 2014.[7] We selected those projects to include a variety of sizes (based on number of returns examined), ages (start dates for the project), as well as some projects that relied on Form 990 data queries and politically sensitive projects. We reviewed the project files for each project to test whether the documentation—such as development and approval of examination selection criteria—followed project development procedures. We also reviewed a non-generalizable sample of 11 closed examination files that originated with whistleblowers to check that IRM and referrals procedures were followed with regard to ensuring whistleblower information is not kept in the examination file. Finally, we interviewed EO officials about the processes and discussed deficiencies we identified.

We designed uniform data collection instruments for our file and database reviews to consistently capture information on the completeness of required documentation and approvals related to case selection. IRS verified the criteria we used in our instruments, and identified any outdated criteria we had

[87] IRM Part 4, Chapter 75, Section 5.6.

[88] We compared the start dates provided by IRS with activity from each committee member documented in the Referrals Database. We found that, in general, the dates IRS provided align with activity recorded in the database.

[89] IRM Part 4, Chapter 75, Section 5.6.

[90] EO drafted a memorandum in February 2014, but it was never issued.

End Notes for Appendix I

[1] A compliance review determines whether an organization is operating in accordance with its exempt purpose and is current with its filing requirements, based on document review and research without direct taxpayer contact. A compliance check is a correspondence contact with an organization to inquire about compliance.

[2] IRM, Part 1, Chapter 1, Section 23.

[3] GAO, *Standards for Internal Control in the Federal Government*, GAO-AIMD-00-21.3 (Washington, D.C., November 1999).

[4] For the six groups of staff who work in the examination selection process, who were located in Ogden, Utah; Dallas; and Atlanta, we were able to invite all staff, with exception of one group where we randomly selected participants in order to have a manageable group size. Staff who conduct examinations are located all over the country. We invited all examination staff based in Dallas for the two relevant focus groups so that we could conduct the groups in person.

[5] The Referral Database contains records of all referrals received in EO, including those that were mistakenly sent to EO (misroutes) and those that do have not have enough information to classify (no issue referrals). For other referrals, the database serves as a log of actions on a referral, including the classification decision and explanation for the decision. In our population and samples, we only reviewed referrals that completed the classification process in fiscal year 2014. We excluded duplicate referrals (referrals on the same issue for an organization), misroutes, and referrals that were still being classified. The EOCA Database contains records of all compliance review and compliance check cases worked by EOCA. We only reviewed cases that were closed in fiscal year 2014. We excluded reviews of operations performed for the Patient Protection and Affordable Care Act because there were no selection decisions related to those reviews. The EOCA Classification Database contains records of all tax returns classified by EOCA. We only reviewed cases that were closed in fiscal year 2014.

[6] Once an examination is sent to an examination group, the manager or examination staff may dismiss the return from examination. Typically, this is done because a return is nearing the date that limits the time period during which IRS may impose taxes or penalties on the return, based on statutory requirements.

[7] EO initiates projects that focus on specific areas of potential noncompliance (such as fundraising) or specific types of organizations (such as community foundations).

End Note for Appendix II

[1]There were a few situations in which we could not make a conclusive determination about whether implementation was successful. We reviewed certain sub-categories of samples, and we did not design our samples to support estimation for these subcategories. Similarly, in the case of examination files that originated with whistleblower referrals, we reviewed a number of files that was not designed to support estimation. Additionally, in some cases, the 95 percent confidence intervals around our estimates overlapped the 5 percent tolerable error rate.

In: IRS Examination …
Editor: Austin H. White

ISBN: 978-1-63484-471-0

Chapter 2

TESTIMONY OF JOHN KOSKINEN, COMMISSIONER, INTERNAL REVENUE SERVICE. HEARING ON "IRS AUDIT SELECTION PROCESS"*

INTRODUCTION

Chairman Roskam, Ranking Member Lewis and Members of the Subcommittee, thank you for the opportunity to appear before you today to discuss the report by the Government Accountability Office (GAO) on the criteria the IRS uses to select exempt organizations for audit.

Let me begin by reiterating my belief that the IRS must continue to do everything possible to ensure that all individuals and organizations can be confident that they will be treated fairly in their dealings with this agency. I would note that the GAO's report on the criteria we use to select exempt organizations for audit found no evidence of organizations being selected in an unfair or biased manner. We welcome the GAO's recommendations for improvements in our processes in order to lower still further the risk of partiality entering into the audit selection process. The actions we are taking in response to those recommendations are discussed in greater detail below.

It is critical for the IRS to continually monitor its processes and procedures and determine where improvements are needed, not just in regard to audits and other compliance activities, but throughout agency operations. To

* This is an edited, reformatted and augmented version of testimony presented July 23, 2015 before the House Committee on Ways and Means, Subcommittee on Oversight.

enhance these capabilities within the IRS, we have established an agency-wide enterprise risk management program, creating risk management liaisons in each area of our operations and providing for the regular identification and analysis of risks to be mitigated or managed. The risk management program builds from and complements existing internal controls and program management activities across the agency.

We are working to further encourage a culture where employees think of themselves as risk managers and understand they should report any issues or problems that occur. My goal is to have employees understand that the only problems we can't solve are the ones we don't know about. As a corollary to that effort, we continue to encourage the flow of information from front line employees up through the organization as well as out to the front line from senior managers.

Recognizing the need to ensure fairness and impartiality in all of the agency's activities, including the exempt organizations area, in 2013 the new IRS Chief Risk Officer – who had been selected from outside the agency – conducted a review of the audit selection criteria used in more than 350 compliance programs across the Service, to identify any instances where there could be a risk of unfairness embedded in that criteria.

I'm pleased to report that the Chief Risk Officer found no evidence of partiality in those programs, and deemed the risk of unfairness entering into these programs in the future to be low, based on the documentary evidence of business rules, procedures, criteria and internal controls reviewed. The Chief Risk Officer did identify a few instances where internal controls could be tightened in order to further reduce the risk of bias, and IRS business units have responded to all of the points he raised.

Ensuring Fairness in EO Compliance Programs

The IRS has a variety of tools at its disposal to make certain that tax-exempt organizations comply with federal tax law. The responsibility for administering these procedures belongs to the Exempt Organizations (EO) function, which is part of the Tax Exempt and Government Entities (TE/GE) Operating Division.

The types of compliance activities that EO conducts in regard to tax exempt organizations fall into two broad categories: audits and compliance checks.

Audits, or examinations, normally include a review of a taxpayer's books and records to determine tax liability, though audits in the tax-exempt area also look at an organization's qualification for tax-exempt status.

EO also conducts compliance checks, which are reviews to determine whether an organization is adhering to recordkeeping and information reporting requirements. In conducting compliance checks, EO specialists may inquire about an item on a return, ask whether specific reporting requirements have been met, or look to see whether an organization's activities are consistent with its stated tax-exempt purpose.

In regard to audits of exempt organizations, EO designs its compliance activities to address issues that carry the most non-compliance risk. We do that by applying data analytics to the wealth of information we receive from Forms 990, *Return of Organization Exempt from income Tax*, which are filed annually by exempt organizations, as well as information from other sources.

Responsibility for developing potential compliance issues and selecting returns for audit falls to the Compliance Strategy Critical Initiatives (CSCI) group within EO. Once the issues are identified, CSCI works to identify the returns that contain the issues in question. The EO Case Selection and Delivery unit (CS&D) is responsible for obtaining the necessary returns to satisfy the requirements of the examination program and transferring the returns to the appropriate examination groups that cover the geographic areas where the organizations are located.

In developing issues and selecting returns for audit, EO also receives referrals from the general public and Congress about potential non-compliance by exempt organizations. These referrals are all handled in a standardized manner no matter what the source. EO maintains three referral committees to review referrals and determine whether examination potential exists. One committee handles referrals regarding churches or houses of worship, a second handles referrals regarding political campaign activity potentially in excess of what is allowed by law, and the third handles referrals with regard to public figures, or institutions that are considered high profile. Each committee is composed of three senior EO staff members – all of whom are career civil servants – on a rotating assignment, and the committees all make decisions about examination potential by majority vote. Referrals not falling into any of the above three categories are reviewed by a classifier rather than a committee.

As noted above, the GAO's report found no examples of EO selecting organizations for audit based on criteria or practices that fall short of TE/GE's stated mission of ensuring fairness and integrity. In its report, the GAO acknowledged that EO's reliance on a variety of sources to select returns for examination shows that EO recognizes the importance of having a robust and effective internal control system to maintain impartiality in the return selection process.

The GAO noted that EO has well-documented procedures for numerous examination selection processes, all of which are contained in the Internal Revenue Manual (IRM), which is our primary, official source of instructions to staff throughout the IRS.

At the same time, the GAO also identified areas where EO's system of internal controls for the audit selection process could be improved in order to reduce the hypothetical risk that exists for returns to be selected in an unfair or biased manner. In response to the GAO's recommendations, we are proceeding with a number of actions to tighten these internal controls, including the following:

Updating the Internal Revenue Manual. A critical part of ensuring fairness, integrity and consistency in the audit selection process involves communicating the appropriate procedures to EO employees, which as noted above is accomplished primarily through the IRM. The GAO identified a number of areas where updates to the IRM are needed. In fact, EO is in the second year of a three-year plan to update all 145 IRM sections pertaining to the EO function. New sections are being created as new processes are put into place. For example, we are currently developing IRM sections for the simplified and streamlined exemption application process and the recently implemented post-determination process.

Specifically related to audits, the EO Examinations office is expected to complete its review and update of 46 of the 62 Examinations IRM sections in Fiscal Year (FY) 2015. The remaining sections are scheduled to be reviewed and updated in FY 2016. EO Examinations is also creating new IRM sections to formalize the guidance on compliance checks and compliance reviews, and to outline the EO Compliance Area classification procedures. It is important to note that, as a practical matter, EO requires adherence to both the IRM and all non-IRM procedure documents that are issued, and the GAO did not identify any evidence of deviation from either source of guidance. Going forward, EO will review and update all pertinent IRM sections on an annual basis.

Expanded monitoring procedures. EO will review its current monitoring procedures to ensure that processes, such as documenting explanations for audit selection decisions and obtaining the necessary sign-offs for those decisions, continue to be followed. The monitoring procedures will be accomplished through operational reviews by the appropriate executives.

These reviews will document whether the appropriate documentation for case selection decisions is maintained and if periodic adjustments are needed. To be clear, classifiers review referrals – which could be complaints from members of the public not versed in tax law – to identify those that contain potential violations of the federal tax laws. Further review of referrals that do not identify federal tax issues would be inefficient and out of scope.

Improved documentation of selection processes. EO Examinations is undertaking efforts to ensure that all criteria used to select returns for examination and executive approvals for added or changed criteria will be documented, including changes that occur during a project or in a new phase of a project. Additionally, IRM sections are being written for examination selection procedures, including a process to ensure the criteria and selection decisions are consistently documented.

Additional training for classifiers. EO will provide cross-training to employees who work with various types of referrals, to improve their ability to correctly select returns for audit from referrals that cover a wide variety of subject matter. EO will prioritize training of classifiers working with political activity, high-profile and church referrals.

Increased tracking and maintenance of closed case files. EO will review and, if necessary, clarify its internal processes for monitoring and shipping case files, and will work with the other business divisions to ensure proper coordination with them in regard to the process of requesting, shipping, tracking and storing closed case files.

Ensuring diversity among referral committee members. EO will change the policy that members of the committees that review referrals for audit participate on a voluntary basis. Historically, the referral committees have been staffed by qualified employees who volunteer for this assignment with the expectation of being relieved of the assignment in 12 months. As committee workload has increased, fewer qualified employees have volunteered for this assignment and, as a result, this has extended the service of committee members. In recognition of this dynamic, EO plans to staff the referral committees by collateral assignment and not through the volunteer process. Thus, participation by EO managers will no longer be voluntary, and we will ensure committee members are rotated on a regular basis.

MAINTAINING IMPARTIALITY THROUGHOUT THE EO FUNCTION

The work being done within EO to ensure fairness and impartiality extends beyond the audit process. The IRS is continuing the efforts it began in 2013 to implement broad managerial and operational improvements in the determination process for tax-exempt status. The IRS has implemented all of the recommendations made by the Treasury Inspector General for Tax Administration in its May 2013 report. The Inspector General reviewed our responses to those recommendations, and in March of this year issued a follow-up report, noting that the IRS has taken "significant actions" to address the 2013 recommendations.

These are important steps. We have eliminated the use of inappropriate criteria; we have expedited the processing of section 501(c)(4) applications; we have instituted a quality review process to ensure that unnecessary or improper information requests are not sent to applicants; and the Department of the Treasury and the IRS have begun the process of revising draft guidance to address how to measure social welfare and non-social welfare activities of section 501(c)(4) organizations. Our goal on this last point is to provide guidance that is clear, fair to everyone, and easy to administer.

The changes we have made in response to the Inspector General's recommendations on exempt organizations also include:

- Establishing a new process for documenting the reasons why applications are chosen for further review during the application process;
- Developing new training and workshops for employees on a number of critical issues, including the difference between issue advocacy and political campaign intervention, and the proper way, under current law, to identify applications that require review of potentially significant political campaign intervention;
- Establishing guidelines for EO specialists on how to process requests for tax-exempt status involving organizations engaging in potentially significant political campaign intervention; and
- Creating a formal, documented process for EO determinations personnel to request assistance from technical experts.

In addition to these actions, the entire leadership chain from the top down to the EO function is new since 2013, starting with the Commissioner of the IRS, the Deputy Commissioner for Services and Enforcement, the Commissioner and Deputy Commissioner of TE/GE, and the Director of the EO function.

One critical area addressed by the new leadership team has been the backlog in pending section 501(c)(4) applications. We have reduced the inventory of section 501(c)(4) applications, including the group of 145 cases in the "priority backlog" – those that were pending for 120 days or more as of May 2013. By July 2, 2015, 140 of those cases, or 97 percent, were closed. Of the closed cases, 107 of them were approved, including 43 organizations that took advantage of a temporary self-certification procedure we offered in summer 2013. Of the remaining 33 closed cases, most were closed without a determination, either because the organization withdrew the application or it failed to respond to our questions. To date, five applications have been denied. The remaining five cases are still open.

CONCLUSION

During my tenure as IRS Commissioner, one of my top priorities has been and continues to be making sure the public understands that anyone – any individual, business or organization – dealing with the IRS will be treated fairly, no matter what their political affiliation, their position on contentious political issues, or whom they supported in the last election.

On the individual side, we will audit over 1 million taxpayers this year. And when someone hears from us regarding their tax return – by letter, I should add, in light of the recent proliferation of IRS impersonation telephone scams – they need to understand that it is only because of something in their tax return, and not other factors. And, if someone else has the same issue on their return, they will hear from us as well, within the limits of our budget resources.

In the exempt organizations area, we will continue to review and improve our efforts to maintain appropriate oversight of, and compliance by, the tax-exempt sector, including our examination case selection internal control system.

Chairman Roskam, Ranking Member Lewis and Members of the Subcommittee, this concludes my statement. I would be happy to take your questions.

In: IRS Examination …
Editor: Austin H. White

ISBN: 978-1-63484-471-0

Chapter 3

TESTIMONY OF MICHELLE EASTON, PRESIDENT, CLARE BOOTHE LUCE POLICY INSTITUTE. HEARING ON "IRS AUDIT SELECTION PROCESS"*

Thank you Chairman Roskam for inviting me to appear before your Subcommittee this morning to tell you about the IRS audit of the Clare Boothe Luce Policy Institute.

I am president of the Clare Boothe Luce Policy Institute a nonprofit educational Section 501(c)(3) tax exempt organization that I founded 22 years ago, with a mission to prepare and promote conservative women leaders. We work primarily with young women in college, some in high school and some who are post-school.

I was a federal government official myself for 12 years -- winning Senate confirmation from a Democrat-controlled U. S. Senate; then served 4 years as a state official in Virginia. I know the responsibility of government first hand and that there is a proper role for investigation. I also know it is possible for government to act inappropriately.

I became an attorney working my way through night law school at American University, graduating in 1980. As part of my Continuing Legal Education I have attended Georgetown University's Nonprofit Tax Seminars -- which in the past often featured Lois Lerner as a speaker. The IRS and Lois Lerner have preached that transparency is part of good non-profit

---

* This is an edited, reformatted and augmented version of testimony presented July 23, 2015 before the House Committee on Ways and Means, Subcommittee on Oversight.

management. But we have come to learn that transparency isn't practiced at the IRS.

I have been extraordinarily careful both as President of the Institute and as an attorney to follow IRS rules for tax exempt organizations, having heard about the horrors of an IRS audit from several other conservative organizations. I was confident I had done everything I was supposed to do.

Nonetheless, in January 2011 -- Happy New Year -- a woman from the IRS telephoned me to say our Form 990 from the fiscal year 2008 had been "selected for examination." She was telling me that the Clare Boothe Luce Policy Institute was going to be subjected to an IRS audit! The IRS agent who called refused to tell me how or why we were selected – that was "private" she said. She claimed the IRS just wanted to insure the activities of the Institute were proper under our tax exempt status.

Now in 2008, the fiscal year the IRS selected for auditing the Institute, I temporarily resigned as President of the Institute, left the staff and our Headquarters office, and went off the payroll for several weeks, to volunteer my time to work for Sarah Palin's candidacy for Vice-President. My work for the Palin campaign was undertaken and executed in consultation with our corporate attorney, taking every precaution to protect the Institute while exercising my First Amendment rights as a citizen.

I never believed that the IRS "randomly" selected the Institute for an audit for the 2008 fiscal year. We have never been given access to any information as to how or why the IRS decided to audit the Clare Boothe Luce Policy Institute – or why the 2008 fiscal year was the focus of our "random" audit. Since neither the public nor Congress has been privy to Lois Lerner's emails, we may never know what she said about the Clare Boothe Luce Policy Institute.

The first part of our audit began with the arrival of two IRS agents at our Virginia Headquarters to conduct an interview of me. The IRS agents asked a series of probing questions like -- what does the Clare Boothe Luce Policy Institute do?

After the interview they asked for a tour of our headquarters. When they came to my office door the male agent spotted a photograph on my office wall of me with President Reagan -- with whom I had the honor of working during the 8 years of his Administration. The agent's eyes widened and his jaw dropped in dismay.

Why would an IRS agent be so shocked and dismayed at a photo of me and a president of the United States?

In the very first of seven separate requests for massive amounts of documents, the IRS asked for a "List of contributors and Amounts."

I would note here that in Lois Lerner's May 2013 admission of wrongdoing, she confessed that the requests to applicants for exempt status for contributor names were not appropriate.

I vigorously objected to releasing to the intrusive IRS auditors the names of our financial supporters. Our donors are such tremendous patriotic Americans, and I knew it was worth the effort to preserve their privacy.

And I am especially glad now that we protected our supporters' privacy since we've learned the IRS leaked information about conservative organizations like the National Organization for Marriage to leftwing advocates, which then used the information to write "slash and burn" stories about conservative supporters of the groups.

To comply with the seven massive document requests from the IRS, the Institute had to provide boxes and boxes and reams of documents. (For example, they made us provide copies of bank statements, list broker statements, check registers, a schedule of accounts payable, a schedule of accounts receivable, credit card statements and on and on.) This took the greater part of 2011 and cost tens of thousands of dollars in attorney, accountant, and staff time to comply with the IRS demands.

And, of course, it kept us doing less of what we exist for -- preparing young women for conservative leadership. I would note that 2011 was, very coincidentally according the IRS, the year before the country was about to select its national leadership.

What other groups that educate people in conservative ideas were randomly selected for audits in 2011 I wonder? It is all a secret with the IRS and it makes a thoughtful person very skeptical.

The IRS auditors must not have found what they were looking for in our 2008 records, because before they had completed the audit of 2008, the IRS then demanded 2009 records as well.

More paper, more time, more money were spent on a random audit, instead of on our mission of preparing and promoting conservative women leaders.

At the end of all this harassment, the IRS concluded initially that while the Institute "continues to qualify for exemption from Federal income tax" that the Institute owed taxes from past years and in future years because the IRS claimed we were operating a list rental business. It was a truly bizarre determination as we have a small staff, we use a mailing company to make list rental decisions for our mailings and have nothing to do with approving or processing list rentals.

After additional thousands of dollars more in legal costs to appeal this finding, we were finally, totally, cleared by the IRS.

Tens of thousands of dollars later, with so much lost opportunity to prepare and promote conservative women leaders, I was in fact right; I had done everything that I should have done, properly and correctly.

To add insult to injury, after all this intrusion and diversion of our precious time and money, in December of 2011 the IRS sent a cheery request that we help them improve their service to the public by answering a questionnaire about their audit. Their letter read "...Your name was selected through a scientific random sampling process to receive this survey because IRS recently completed an examination (audit) of your organization. We want to know your opinions regarding that experience and the service you received from IRS. Your responses are critical to the accuracy of this evaluation ...."

I told our attorney "I want to eliminate the IRS, not help improve their service." Our attorney told me that this was the one communication from the IRS to which I had no obligation to respond.

The May 2013 admission by the IRS was shocking. You may recall Tax Exempt Division Director Lois Lerner had planted a question with her friend -- about IRS handling of Tea Party exemption applications. Lerner admitted publicly that the actions by the IRS against these conservative groups were “absolutely inappropriate.” I immediately called our attorney and said I want to go public now to discuss our harassing audit, and he said, “Go right ahead Ð someone has to fight back.”

Many organizations, however, do not want it known that they have been selected for an audit. Or that they spent tens of thousands of dollars of donor funds defending an audit. Or that the IRS examined not just one year, but two.

Have any of you or your family or business been subject to an IRS audit? Ð How did you feel about the audit? Pretty proud about that? If I leave you with no other thought, please let it be this:

If the great majority of IRS audits are truly random, as the IRS claims, the IRS should publish on January 1 a list of all the groups and individuals that they plan to do these random audits on through the year.

Then, we could see if the audits are truly random, or whether they are focused on those nonprofits which oppose the policies of the incumbent Administration. If Lois Lerner had been required to be transparent, the public would have been able to see much sooner whether her selection of nonprofit organizations to audit was truly random as she claimed – until she finally owned up to her serious "inappropriate" selection criteria.

And, at least, then the stigma would be gone – "hey, it is just my bad luck to be selected for a random audit." Then the motivation that many nonprofits feel to keep an IRS audit a secret is gone. You don't need to worry about your supporters thinking you are doing something wrong if they find out about the audit. All those negatives that automatically come with an audit would be gone.

The IRS should be required to publish the list of their random audits to take away the mystery.

These are outrageous abuses of governmental power. Even though Lois Lerner and her apologists are still trying to hide what happened, there is every reason to believe that the IRS has abused its power over nonprofits. As this IRS scandal continues, with the perpetrators still unpunished, citizens lose confidence in their government and are reluctant to cooperate with government enforcement. When you see open hostility and disrespect from a government agent looking at a picture of me and President Reagan, you get the sense they exercise governmental power less like umpires and more like partisans. This is truly corrosive to good governance.

This experience with the IRS illustrates what we at the Clare Boothe Luce Policy Institute have been teaching young people for decades – just how far we have come from the vision of the founding fathers who viewed citizens as the masters, and government workers as their servants.

The Clare Boothe Luce Policy Institute is a growing and influential conservative organization with unique outreach to women through our annual Great American Conservative Women calendar, our Woman of the Year and other awards for Conservative Women, our campus lecture program, conferences, seminars and our various other programs effectively preparing young conservative women for greater leadership.

Over the past couple of years, hearing of the IRS abuses of other conservative groups, I wanted to share our organization's experience with IRS abuse with you.

But I hope that Members of this Sub-Committee who do not agree with our conservative message would be equally outraged by IRS abuses. If the IRS under the Obama Administration can go after conservative organizations, then the precedent would be established for the IRS to be used to achieve partisan, political objectives under any Administration -- completely ending anything resembling the rule of law at the IRS.

In: IRS Examination …
Editor: Austin H. White
ISBN: 978-1-63484-471-0

Chapter 4

TESTIMONY OF ELIZABETH J. KINGSLEY, PARTNER, HARMON, CURRAN, SPIELBERG & EISENBERG, LLP. HEARING ON "IRS AUDIT SELECTION PROCESS"*

Chairman Roskam, Ranking Member Lewis, and Members of the Subcommittee, thank you for the opportunity to testify here today.

By way of background, I am an attorney with the law firm of Harmon, Curran, Spielberg & Eisenberg, LLP. We are a small firm that is primarily dedicated to representing nonprofit organizations.[1] While many of our clients are not politically active, and some are consciously non- or bi-partisan, the politically engaged groups we work with are predominantly progressive. What I want to talk about today is what I have seen in recent years of these groups' experience with IRS audits.

OVERVIEW -- IRS AUDIT ACTIVITY

Over the years, the Exempt Organizations division of the IRS has maintained the functions of education, guidance, compliance and enforcement. However, the emphasis and resources allocated to each of those functions varies. In my two decades of practice, I have seen that pendulum move back and forth several times.[2]

---

* This is an edited, reformatted and augmented version of testimony presented July 23, 2015 before the House Committee on Ways and Means, Subcommittee on Oversight.

In the early years of this century, the IRS conducted a "Political Activity Compliance Initiative," to investigate allegations of section 501(c)(3) organizations apparently violating the prohibition on intervention in campaigns on behalf of or in opposition to candidates for public office to which those organizations are subject. This was a systematic attempt to provide a mechanism to handle reports of charities engaging in political campaign intervention on an expedited basis during an election year. In one form or another, this PACI program was in effect for the 2004, 2006, and 2008 federal election years. Reports were issued after each cycle.

With the release of the FY 2011 work plan, review of allegations of political campaign intervention was moved "from project to process" and no further reports have been forthcoming. After this transition, there was very little evidence that nonprofits were being audited even for blatant violations of the campaign intervention prohibition. I regularly attend meetings of the ABA Tax Section, and specifically its Exempt Organizations Committee. At breakfast meetings of the Subcommittee on Politics and Lobbying Activities, we would regularly ask the attendees whether anyone was handling or had heard of any audits inquiring into improper political activity. From 2009 into mid-2012, no one reported any indications of such audits occurring. While this was not a scientific survey and cannot be taken as definitive proof, it would be surprising if there had been a substantial political activities audit program under way and none of the examinations had come to the attention of that group of lawyers who specialize in that particular area of tax law.

More recently, the Service has speeded up processing of exemption applications in order to clear a serious backlog. IRS officials have also publicly stated that they plan to devote resources to following up after the exemption determinations are issued to ensure organizations are complying with the constraints imposed by the kind of tax exemption they enjoy. We have certainly seen that at my firm. My assessment indicates that we have handled more audits in the past five years than in the preceding fifteen. Our colleagues at the ABA meetings have reported a similar increase in audit activity, starting in late 2012 or early 2013.

Our Recent Audit Experiences

In the past few years we have seen at least nine audits of organizations that can reasonably be described as progressive. These have included both 501(c)(3) and 501(c)(4) groups. They have ranged from small to mid-sized, with budgets from less than $100,000 to approximately $3,000,000. The groups selected for audit have included those that lobby for or otherwise promote progressive policy changes, some that affirmatively advocate for progressive political candidates, some that support civic engagement at the grassroots level, and others that conduct data-intensive research on technical policy issues. Some audits have grown out of complaints from ideological opponents, some we were told have been just selected randomly, and in at least one case we suspect the audit was triggered by specific information in the Form 990 that was filed.

Even for the most well-run organization that is confident of its fundamental tax compliance, an IRS audit is disruptive and alarming. It draws time and energy away from working on the mission. Audits are inherently intrusive and usually expensive. In contrast to audits of individuals or for-profit businesses, an examination of a tax-exempt organization can be especially intrusive. The auditor needs to look not only at whether taxes (such as payroll taxes or unrelated business income tax) have been paid as required, but whether the entity still qualifies for tax-exemption. This entails an in-depth examination of activities to verify that the organization's operations further the purposes for which it was granted exemption. For a 501(c)(3) organization this means demonstrating that it does not engage in any political campaign intervention and does not exceed the limited amount of lobbying it is allowed to do; for a 501(c)(4) group it means demonstrating that it is primarily operated for qualifying social welfare purposes, and political campaign intervention and other activities do not outstrip those social welfare activities. Financial records are only a part of the picture.

Costs can vary widely. Our firm's clients tend to be small to mid-sized organizations that are very budget-conscious. We have a commitment as a firm to helping these groups receive legal representation that they might not otherwise be able to afford. Consequently we work hard to keep our rates as low as possible, and we try to be flexible in how we provide our advice, and depending on the situation and the organization our involvement in the audit process may be limited in order to keep costs down. However, even the most minimalist approach will generate thousands of dollars in legal and accounting fees, not to mention the costs of staff time devoted to the process. A more typical audit can easily run to tens of thousands of dollars -- and that's when the whole thing goes perfectly smoothly, with only one visit from the auditor, one set of document requests, and no major issues raised that must be addressed.

An audit is typically initiated by a letter accompanied by a list of documents that the auditor wants to see. These can run to many pages, with multiple requests per page. In addition to detailed financial information, requests we have seen include:

- Minutes of meetings of governing body, including committees from January 1, 2010 to present
- All correspondence files of the organization with the IRS
- Copies of pamphlets, brochures, magazines, newsletters, programs, membership application, and other literature printed
- Manual of Standard Operating Procedures
- Contracts, leases, agreements etc. (including contracts for services)
- List of project managers, projects worked on, and compensation paid
- List of consulting agreements entered into, name of consultant, compensation paid, and copies of the consultant's work product
- Conflict of Interest statement
- Provide information on travel reimbursement policy/procedures
- Provide information on all agreements and transactions the organization has had, either directly or indirectly with any substantial contributor, trustees, directors, officers, creators, key employees, or members of their families, or with any taxable organization with which any such person is affiliated.
- Copy of Grant applications submitted to charities/foundations in which you received funding
    - Provide information on grant requirements
    - Provide final financial accounting for the grant funds received
    - Evaluation and summary of the results obtained from grant funds received

An auditor's first visit can last days and can stretch over several weeks. It is often followed by additional requests for information. Typically these focus on areas the auditor has determined are of particular interest (e.g., one client was asked for details about credit card use), but often they can be burdensome and expensive to comply with.

From beginning to end the process will take months, and can take years. Even when everything goes perfectly smoothly and the auditor does not identify issues or concerns, I seldom see an audit wrap up in much less than a year. Two years is not unheard of. It is common that an auditor requests that the taxpayer agree to extend the statute of limitations in order for them to complete their work. To be sure, the audit is not active for this entire period. Examiners typically have multiple cases open, and can be called away for other purposes such as training. However, for the organization, there is an open IRS audit hanging over their heads for what often seems an excruciatingly long time.

AN ILLUSTRATIVE EXAMPLE -- PROJECT VOTE

To illustrate how this process can play out, let me tell you the story of an audit of my client Project Vote. Project Vote is a national, nonpartisan, nonprofit organization founded on the belief that an organized, diverse electorate is the key to a better America. Its mission is to build an electorate that accurately represents the diversity of this nation's citizenry, and to ensure that every eligible citizen can register, vote, and cast a ballot that counts. Since 1994, Project Vote has worked to increase voter registration and participation among historically underrepresented citizens, and has emerged in recent years as a national leader in voting rights.

In 2012, the organization received notice that the IRS was going to audit it for the year 2010. We learned that the basis for the audit was not random but that it was triggered by a complaint filed by a disgruntled former employee. One might expect such a complaint to be discounted when filed by a person with an obvious ax to grind, but in this case it was considered sufficient basis to open an exam.[3]

The initial audit letter was sent in April, 2012, and our first meeting with the examiner was held in June of that year. Although the audit was for FY 2010, in the process Project Vote was asked to extend the statute of limitations for 2008 while the examiner decided whether or not to open an audit of that year as well. Upon consideration the organization reluctantly agreed, judging it better to allow the auditor the time to realize that such further inquiry would not be a good use of resources rather than having to make the decision under pressure of looming expiration of the statute of limitations.

The first set of document requests in this audit ran to six pages and generated over 1 GB of data, containing more than three thousand pages. This was followed in August, 2012 by another request for eight different types of information.

The audit was open for more than two years, and cost the organization over $20,000 in legal and accounting fees, plus untold hours of staff time diverted to handle the matter. It eventually was closed in July, 2014 with a letter indicating that the organization's exempt status continued and it was not subject to any excise taxes or other tax liabilities.

Although Project Vote's activities are scrupulously nonpartisan, because it seeks to engage historically disenfranchised populations in our nation's civic life, it is perceived to be politically progressive. The fact that it, too, was subject to a lengthy, expensive, and intrusive IRS audit provides evidence that the agency is not targeting its audit resources on a politically biased basis.

End Notes

[1] While I advise and represent many different clients, I am appearing today solely on my own behalf. Although some client organizations have given me permission to talk about their experiences with IRS audits, in presenting this testimony I am representing only myself.

[2] To be precise, I have seen the precedential guidance released dwindle to a barely perceptible trickle, but the balance between education and enforcement has shifted.

[3] The employee was fired for dishonest conduct –use of a credit card for unauthorized personal expenses.

INDEX

A

B

C

H

I

J

L

M

N

O